Table of Contents

Introduction: The Ultimate Tariffs Survival Guide

Summary of Key Points 4

Defining Tariffs and Their Historical Significance 5

The Impact of Tariffs on Businesses, Consumers, and Global Trade 7

Why Understanding Tariffs Is Crucial for Survival in Today's Economic Landscape 9

What Are Tariffs? 11

Why Are Tariffs Imposed? 13

Real-World Examples of Major Tariffs and Their Consequences 15

For Businesses 18

For Consumers 20

Case Studies: Winners and Losers in Tariff Wars 22

The Role of Tariffs in International Trade Agreements (e.g., NAFTA, WTO) 27

How Different Countries Respond to Tariffs 32

Conclusion 36

The Ripple Effects of Major Tariff Disputes on Global Supply Chains 37

Conclusion 42

Strategies for Minimizing Impact of Tariffs 43

Conclusion 46

Financial Planning: 47

Conclusion 49

Tools and Technologies for Tracking and Managing Tariff Changes 50

Conclusion 54

How to Identify Tariff-Inflated Prices 55

Conclusion 58

Strategies for Saving Money: Alternative Brands, Local Goods, and More 60

Conclusion 64

Advocating for Fair Trade Practices 65

Merging Trends in Global Trade Policies 70

Conclusion 75

The Potential for New Tariffs in Key Industries (e.g., Tech, Agriculture) 76

How Businesses and Consumers Can Stay Informed and Adapt 80

Case Studies of Businesses That Thrived Despite Tariffs ... 85

Conclusion 89

Lessons Learned from Past Tariff Battles 90

Conclusion 94

A Step-by-Step Guide for Businesses 95

A Step-by-Step Guide for Consumers 101

Conclusion 105

Appendices 107

Introduction: The Ultimate Tariffs Survival Guide

In the interconnected web of global trade, tariffs act as both a tool and a barrier. At their core, tariffs are taxes or duties imposed by governments on imported or exported goods. Historically, tariffs have played a pivotal role in shaping economies and influencing international relations. From the protective tariffs of the Industrial Revolution to the trade wars of the modern era, these economic instruments have left a profound mark on the world stage.

The impact of tariffs is far-reaching, affecting everyone from multinational corporations to everyday consumers. For businesses, tariffs can disrupt supply chains, inflate production costs, and hinder competitiveness in foreign markets. For consumers, they often translate to higher prices and fewer choices on store shelves. On a global scale, tariffs can strain diplomatic relations, fuel economic inequality, and alter the delicate balance of international trade.

Understanding tariffs is no longer optional—it's a necessity. In an era of trade wars, shifting policies, and unpredictable economic landscapes, businesses and consumers alike must equip themselves with the knowledge to adapt and thrive. This survival guide provides the tools and insights to navigate the challenges posed by tariffs, ensuring resilience and success in a world shaped by trade dynamics.

Summary of Key Points

1. **Define Tariffs and Their Historical Significance**
   - Tariffs are taxes on imports or exports, historically used to protect domestic industries, generate revenue, and influence trade relations. They have played a central role in shaping economies and international policies.
2. **The Impact of Tariffs on Businesses, Consumers, and Global Trade**
   - Businesses face higher costs, disrupted supply chains, and challenges in global competitiveness. Consumers experience price increases and limited product availability, while tariffs often escalate global trade tensions and disrupt markets.
3. **The Importance of Understanding Tariffs for Survival**
   - In today's volatile economic climate, staying informed about tariffs is critical for navigating risks, seizing opportunities, and maintaining stability in personal finances and business operations.

Defining Tariffs and Their Historical Significance

Tariffs are taxes or duties imposed by a government on imported or exported goods. Their primary purpose is to regulate trade by either encouraging or discouraging the movement of goods across borders. By increasing the cost of foreign goods, tariffs can protect domestic industries from international competition, generate government revenue, or influence foreign trade policies.

Historically, tariffs have been instrumental in shaping national economies and global trade dynamics. In the 18th and 19th centuries, protective tariffs were used to shield fledgling industries in countries like the United States and Germany, enabling them to grow without the threat of established international competitors. The Tariff of 1828 in the United States, also known as the "Tariff of Abominations," is a well-known example, as it sparked heated debates about economic policy and regional tensions leading up to the Civil War.

Globally, tariffs have often been at the center of economic conflict. The infamous Smoot-Hawley Tariff Act of 1930, which raised U.S. tariffs to record levels, is widely cited as exacerbating the Great Depression by stifling international trade. More recently, the U.S.-China trade war has highlighted how tariffs are still used as a strategic tool in geopolitical and economic battles.

The historical significance of tariffs lies in their dual role as both a driver of economic growth and a catalyst for conflict. While they have helped nations establish industrial strength, they have also been responsible for trade disputes, economic downturns, and shifts in global alliances. Understanding this history is crucial for grasping the complexities of tariffs and their continuing influence on the modern world.

The Impact of Tariffs on Businesses, Consumers, and Global Trade

Tariffs create ripple effects that touch nearly every aspect of the economy, influencing businesses, consumers, and the global trade ecosystem.

For businesses, tariffs can significantly increase the cost of importing goods or raw materials, cutting into profit margins. Manufacturers relying on foreign components may find themselves paying more for essential supplies, leading to higher production costs. Exporters can also face retaliatory tariffs, making their products less competitive in international markets. Small and medium-sized enterprises (SMEs) often lack the financial resilience to absorb these additional costs, forcing some to reduce operations, lay off workers, or even shut down.

When businesses face higher costs due to tariffs, those expenses are often passed on to consumers in the form of higher prices. This can lead to inflation and reduced purchasing power, particularly for essential goods like food, clothing, and electronics. Consumers may also encounter limited product availability as businesses cut back on imports or shift to less diverse supply chains. The cumulative effect can strain household budgets and reduce overall quality of life.

Tariffs disrupt the flow of goods across borders, destabilizing global supply chains and creating inefficiencies in the market. When countries impose tariffs on each other, it can lead to trade wars, as seen in recent U.S.-China disputes. These conflicts often escalate, causing uncertainty for businesses and investors worldwide. Tariffs can also lead to a reshuffling of global trade alliances, as nations seek new partners to bypass tariff-heavy markets.

In essence, while tariffs may serve short-term goals like protecting domestic industries or generating revenue, their long-term consequences can include economic instability, reduced consumer welfare, and strained international relations. The interconnected nature of the global economy ensures that the effects of tariffs are rarely confined to the nations that impose them.

Why Understanding Tariffs Is Crucial for Survival in Today's Economic Landscape

In an era of global interconnectedness, tariffs play an outsized role in shaping economic policies, business strategies, and consumer behavior. As governments adjust trade policies to reflect domestic and international priorities, the impact of tariffs reverberates across industries and borders. Understanding tariffs is no longer a niche concern—it is a critical skill for navigating today's volatile economic landscape.

Tariffs can drastically alter a company's operational costs, supply chain dynamics, and market competitiveness. Businesses that fail to anticipate tariff changes may face unexpected expenses, disrupted imports or exports, and even loss of market share. By understanding tariffs, companies can develop strategies to mitigate these risks—such as diversifying suppliers, exploring alternative markets, or renegotiating contracts. Proactive planning allows businesses to remain agile and competitive, even in the face of sudden policy shifts.

For individuals, tariffs directly influence the cost and availability of goods. From grocery bills to electronics purchases, the effects of tariffs are felt in daily life. By staying informed, consumers can make smarter financial decisions, such as supporting local products or timing purchases to avoid price hikes. Understanding tariffs also empowers consumers to advocate for fair trade practices and policies that align with their values.

On a macroeconomic level, tariffs influence trade relationships, economic growth, and geopolitical stability. Being aware of how tariffs impact the global economy enables policymakers, investors, and businesses to make informed decisions that foster resilience and innovation. It also prepares them to adapt to the ripple effects of tariff disputes or trade wars.

In a world where trade policies are increasingly used as tools of diplomacy and competition, understanding tariffs is a survival skill. Whether navigating the complexities of international trade as a business leader or managing household finances as a consumer, staying informed about tariffs ensures preparedness and adaptability in a rapidly changing economic environment.

Chapter 1: The Basics of Tariffs

What Are Tariffs?

Tariffs are taxes or duties imposed by a government on goods as they cross international borders, either when entering (imports) or leaving (exports) a country. They serve as tools to regulate trade, protect domestic industries, and generate government revenue. While tariffs can have positive goals, they often come with unintended economic consequences, such as higher prices for consumers or strained international trade relations.

1. **Import Tariffs**
     - **Definition**: Taxes imposed on goods brought into a country.
     - **Purpose**: To protect domestic industries by making imported goods more expensive compared to locally produced items.
     - **Example**: A country imposes a 20% tariff on imported steel to encourage local steel production.
2. **Export Tariffs**
     - **Definition**: Taxes levied on goods leaving a country.
     - **Purpose**: To restrict exports, keep certain goods in the domestic market, or capitalize on a commodity's high demand abroad.
     - **Example**: A nation imposes an export tariff on rare minerals to ensure sufficient supply for its own industries.

3. **Protective Tariffs**
    - **Definition**: Tariffs designed specifically to shield domestic industries from foreign competition.
    - **Purpose**: To give local businesses a competitive edge by raising the cost of imported alternatives.
    - **Example**: A government imposes a 50% tariff on imported agricultural products to protect its farmers from cheaper foreign produce.
4. **Revenue-Generating Tariffs**
    - **Definition**: Tariffs aimed at generating income for the government rather than protecting industries.
    - **Purpose**: To provide an additional source of national revenue, often in countries with limited domestic production.
    - **Example**: A flat tariff of 10% is imposed on all imported consumer goods to contribute to government funds.

By understanding the definitions and purposes of these types of tariffs, individuals and businesses can better navigate the complexities of international trade and prepare for their potential impacts.

Why Are Tariffs Imposed?

Tariffs are powerful tools used by governments to achieve a variety of goals. While their primary purpose is to regulate trade, their motivations extend beyond economics into the realms of politics and social strategy. Understanding these motivations can shed light on why tariffs are implemented and how they shape national and global dynamics.

- **Strengthening Domestic Industries**: Tariffs are often imposed to protect key industries deemed vital to national security or economic stability. By making imports more expensive, governments encourage domestic production and reduce reliance on foreign suppliers.
- **Trade Negotiations**: Tariffs can serve as leverage in diplomatic negotiations. Countries may impose tariffs to pressure trading partners into favorable agreements or to address perceived unfair trade practices.
- **Retaliation**: In trade disputes, tariffs are frequently used as retaliatory measures. For example, if one country imposes tariffs on another, the affected nation might respond with its own tariffs to restore balance or exert pressure.

- **Revenue Generation**: Tariffs provide a source of income for governments, especially in developing countries where other tax collection systems may be less efficient. Revenue from tariffs can fund infrastructure, social programs, or other public services.
- **Balancing Trade Deficits**: Tariffs can reduce a nation's trade deficit by discouraging imports and encouraging domestic consumption of locally produced goods.
- **Encouraging Economic Growth**: Protecting emerging industries through tariffs—often called "infant industry protection"—allows them to develop and compete on a

global scale without being overwhelmed by established foreign competitors.

- **Job Protection**: By reducing competition from imported goods, tariffs help sustain local industries and preserve jobs. This can be particularly significant in sectors vulnerable to outsourcing or cheaper foreign labor.
- **Promoting National Identity**: In some cases, tariffs are used to encourage citizens to "buy local," fostering a sense of national pride and self-reliance.
- **Addressing Social Priorities**: Tariffs can reflect societal values, such as discouraging imports produced under unethical labor conditions or imposing duties on environmentally harmful products.

In practice, tariffs often serve multiple motivations simultaneously. A tariff might aim to protect domestic jobs, generate revenue, and influence political negotiations, all while promoting broader economic goals. However, these motivations can sometimes conflict, resulting in unintended consequences that impact businesses, consumers, and global trade relations.

Real-World Examples of Major Tariffs and Their Consequences

Tariffs have historically played a pivotal role in shaping economies and influencing international relations. Their consequences—both intended and unintended—offer valuable insights into the complex dynamics of global trade. Here are some notable examples:

- **What Happened**: The United States implemented this tariff to protect domestic farmers and manufacturers during the Great Depression by raising duties on over 20,000 imported goods.
- **Consequences**:
    - Other countries retaliated with their own tariffs, leading to a sharp decline in global trade.
    - International trade volume fell by more than 60%, exacerbating the economic downturn.
    - The tariff is widely criticized for deepening the Great Depression and fueling protectionist policies worldwide.

- **What Happened**: The U.S. imposed tariffs on hundreds of billions of dollars' worth of Chinese goods, citing unfair trade practices and intellectual property theft. China responded with retaliatory tariffs on U.S. exports.
- **Consequences**:
    - Disrupted global supply chains, especially in technology and agriculture.
    - Increased costs for U.S. businesses and consumers, with studies estimating the tariffs cost American households hundreds of dollars annually.
    - Accelerated China's push for self-reliance in industries like semiconductors and green technology.

- **What Happened**: The EU introduced this tariff on imports of carbon-intensive goods like steel and cement to align with its climate change goals.
- **Consequences**:
    - Encouraged trading partners to adopt greener manufacturing practices to remain competitive.
    - Sparked debates over whether the tariff constitutes an environmental initiative or protectionism in disguise.
    - Highlighted the growing influence of environmental concerns in shaping global trade policies.

- **What Happened**: India imposes high tariffs on agricultural imports, including a 60% duty on wheat and 50% on apples, to protect its vast farming sector.
- **Consequences**:
    - Shielded local farmers from international competition, preserving rural livelihoods.
    - Limited foreign access to India's agricultural market, straining trade relationships with countries like the U.S. and Australia.
    - Contributed to higher food prices for Indian consumers during periods of domestic shortages.

- **What Happened**: In response to U.S. tariffs on Canadian steel and aluminum, Canada imposed counter-tariffs on a range of American goods, including steel, aluminum, and consumer products like ketchup and whiskey.
- **Consequences**:
    - Strained trade relations between the two long-standing allies.
    - Increased production costs for Canadian businesses reliant on U.S. metals.
    - Strengthened calls for diversifying trade partnerships beyond the U.S.

These examples illustrate that while tariffs can achieve short-term objectives like protecting industries or advancing strategic goals, they often come with significant trade-offs. Understanding these outcomes is essential for businesses, policymakers, and consumers to navigate the complex landscape of international trade.

Chapter 2: How Tariffs Impact Businesses and Consumers

For Businesses

Tariffs on imported goods often lead to higher costs for businesses that rely on foreign raw materials or components. For instance, a manufacturing company that sources steel from overseas may face significant price hikes due to tariffs, increasing production costs. These expenses are frequently passed on to consumers, making products more expensive and reducing demand. Alternatively, businesses may absorb the costs, which can cut into profit margins and hinder growth.

This issue is especially pronounced in industries with limited domestic suppliers. Companies may struggle to find affordable alternatives, forcing them to make tough decisions about pricing, production, or workforce adjustments. For example, during the U.S.-China trade war, American manufacturers dependent on Chinese components faced steep tariffs that disrupted supply chains and added financial strain.

Tariffs can create an uneven playing field in international trade. When domestic businesses face higher costs due to tariffs, their products may become less competitive abroad. This is particularly problematic for export-driven industries that rely on competitive pricing to penetrate foreign markets.

For example, if a country imposes tariffs on imported parts used in manufacturing finished goods, domestic exporters may struggle to compete with foreign companies that have access to cheaper materials. This can lead to a loss of market share, reduced revenues, and even layoffs.

Furthermore, retaliatory tariffs imposed by other countries can exacerbate the problem. Businesses may find their products targeted by foreign tariffs, further reducing demand for exports. For instance, during trade disputes, agricultural producers often face reduced market access due to retaliatory tariffs on goods like soybeans or dairy products.

In both cases, understanding the potential impacts of tariffs enables businesses to develop mitigation strategies, such as diversifying suppliers, exploring alternative markets, or investing in localized production to reduce exposure to tariff-related risks.

For Consumers

One of the most direct effects of tariffs on consumers is the increase in the prices of goods. When tariffs are imposed on imports, businesses often pass the added costs onto their customers to maintain profitability. This means everyday items—from electronics and clothing to food and household goods—can become significantly more expensive.

For example, during the U.S.-China trade war, tariffs on Chinese imports led to price hikes on products like smartphones, washing machines, and even children's toys. These price increases can strain household budgets, especially for lower-income families who are disproportionately affected by rising costs.

In addition, tariffs on raw materials such as steel or aluminum can indirectly raise prices on a wide range of goods, including cars and construction materials, further impacting consumers in multiple sectors.

Tariffs can also restrict the availability of certain products. When tariffs make imported goods too expensive, businesses may choose to discontinue importing those items altogether. As a result, consumers face fewer choices in the marketplace, which can affect their access to quality, variety, and affordability.

For instance, if a country imposes high tariffs on specialty foods or luxury items, retailers may stop offering those products to avoid the added costs, leaving consumers without access to unique or foreign goods they once enjoyed. Similarly, tariffs on electronic components could delay the release of new technology products, limiting consumer access to cutting-edge innovations.

In some cases, domestic alternatives may fill the gap, but they might not meet the same quality standards or may come at a higher price. For consumers, this can mean sacrificing preferences or paying a premium for goods that were previously more affordable and widely available.

Understanding these impacts highlights the importance of tariffs not just for businesses and governments but also for the everyday consumer navigating a changing economic landscape.

Case Studies: Winners and Losers in Tariff Wars

Tariff wars, often sparked by economic or political disagreements, create a clear divide between those who benefit and those who suffer. The following case studies highlight key examples of winners and losers in recent and historical tariff conflicts, showcasing the diverse and far-reaching consequences of such policies.

Case Study 1: U.S.-China Trade War (2018–Present)

Winners:

- **Domestic U.S. Steel and Aluminum Industries**:
    - The U.S. imposed tariffs on Chinese steel and aluminum to protect domestic producers. Some American steel companies reported increased profits as the tariffs raised the price of imported alternatives, enabling them to capture a larger share of the domestic market.
    - Small towns reliant on steel mills saw temporary boosts in employment and production.

Losers:

- **American Farmers**:
    - China retaliated with tariffs on U.S. agricultural exports, particularly soybeans, pork, and corn. This led to significant losses for American farmers, who struggled to find alternative markets for their products.
    - The U.S. government provided billions of dollars in subsidies to offset the damage, but many farms faced financial ruin.

- **Consumers and Retailers**:
    - Tariffs on Chinese imports raised prices on everyday goods, from clothing to electronics, hurting consumers and small businesses that relied on affordable supply chains.

Case Study 2: Smoot-Hawley Tariff Act (1930)

Winners:

- **A Few Protected U.S. Industries**:
    - The agricultural and manufacturing sectors initially saw marginal benefits as the tariffs raised the cost of competing imports. However, these gains were short-lived.

Losers:

- **Global Trade and U.S. Economy**:
    - Other nations imposed retaliatory tariffs on U.S. exports, leading to a collapse in global trade by over 60%.
    - American industries dependent on exports suffered catastrophic declines, contributing to higher unemployment, and deepening the Great Depression.

Case Study 3: India's Tariffs on Technology Imports (2017)

Winners:

- **Local Electronics Manufacturers:**
    - To boost its domestic manufacturing sector, India imposed tariffs on imported smartphones and electronic components. Companies like Samsung and Foxconn responded by expanding local production facilities to avoid the tariffs, creating jobs, and stimulating the local economy.
- **Government Revenue:**
    - The tariffs provided additional income for the Indian government, funding public projects and initiatives.

Losers:

- **Consumers:**
    - The tariffs raised the price of smartphones and electronics, making them less accessible to average consumers, particularly in rural and low-income areas.
- **Foreign Manufacturers:**
    - Companies reliant on exporting products to India faced declining revenues and were forced to adjust their pricing or market strategies.

Case Study 4: Canada's Retaliatory Tariffs on U.S. Goods (2018)

Winners:

- **Canadian Domestic Producers**:
    - Industries producing goods targeted by U.S. tariffs (such as steel and aluminum) saw temporary boosts in demand domestically, as Canadian businesses turned to local suppliers.

Losers:

- **Canadian Consumers and Businesses**:
    - The retaliatory tariffs imposed by Canada on U.S. goods, including ketchup, whiskey, and steel, led to price increases for consumers.
    - Canadian businesses reliant on U.S. materials faced higher costs, reducing competitiveness and profitability.

Key Takeaways:

- **Winners**: Often include domestic industries protected by tariffs, local manufacturers benefiting from reduced competition, and governments gaining revenue or leveraging tariffs in trade negotiations.
- **Losers**: Typically include consumers facing higher prices, exporters caught in retaliatory measures, and industries reliant on global supply chains.

By examining these case studies, it becomes clear that the outcomes of tariff wars are rarely one-sided, with ripple effects that extend well beyond their intended targets.

Chapter 3: Tariffs in a Global Economy

The Role of Tariffs in International Trade Agreements (e.g., NAFTA, WTO)

Tariffs play a significant role in shaping international trade agreements. These agreements are designed to reduce barriers to trade, promote economic cooperation, and ensure fair competition among nations. Tariffs, while still present, are often the subject of negotiation in such agreements. Below, we explore how tariffs are integrated into some of the most influential international trade frameworks, such as NAFTA (now USMCA) and the World Trade Organization (WTO).

1. NAFTA (North American Free Trade Agreement) - Now USMCA (United States-Mexico-Canada Agreement)

Role of Tariffs in NAFTA/USMCA:

- **Elimination of Tariffs**:
    - One of the core objectives of NAFTA was to reduce tariffs between the U.S., Canada, and Mexico, creating a more integrated market for goods and services. Over the 15 years following NAFTA's implementation in 1994, many tariffs on agricultural, industrial, and consumer goods were eliminated, facilitating increased trade between the three nations.
    - For example, tariffs on agricultural products like corn, wheat, and poultry were phased out, benefiting farmers and food producers.

- **Protecting Sensitive Industries**:
    - Although NAFTA eliminated many tariffs, it also allowed countries to maintain certain protective tariffs in sensitive sectors, like dairy in Canada or textiles in Mexico. These provisions were designed to prevent the influx of cheaper imports that could harm local industries.
    - Under the USMCA, some of these protections were maintained or adjusted, such as the updated rules of origin for automobile manufacturing, ensuring that more components are sourced from within North America.

Impact of Tariffs in NAFTA/USMCA:

- **Increased Trade:**
    o The reduction of tariffs led to an explosion in trade across the region, with trade between the three countries tripling by 2020.
    o U.S. exports to Canada and Mexico increased significantly, benefiting both consumers (through lower prices) and producers (through expanded market access).

- **Dispute Resolution:**
    o NAFTA also included provisions for resolving trade disputes, allowing member nations to challenge the imposition of tariffs or unfair trade practices. The USMCA continues this tradition, with updated rules to better address modern trade issues.

2. WTO (World Trade Organization)

Role of Tariffs in WTO:

- **Global Trade Liberalization:**
    o The WTO, established in 1995, aims to promote free trade by reducing tariffs and other trade barriers between member countries. The WTO works to ensure that international trade flows as smoothly, predictably, and freely as possible.
    o Under the General Agreement on Tariffs and Trade (GATT), the WTO's predecessor, member countries agreed to lower tariffs

through successive rounds of negotiations. The most significant of these was the Uruguay Round, which led to the creation of the WTO itself.

- **Most-Favored-Nation (MFN) Principle**:
    o One of the fundamental principles of the WTO is the Most-Favored-Nation (MFN) principle, which stipulates that if a country reduces tariffs on goods from one member, it must offer the same reduction to all other WTO members. This ensures that no country is discriminated against and promotes equal access to global markets.

- **Tariff Reductions through Trade Rounds**:
    o Since its formation, the WTO has facilitated numerous trade rounds where member countries negotiate tariff reductions, with the goal of gradually opening markets worldwide. For instance, the Doha Round, though stalled, aimed to reduce tariffs on agricultural products to help developing nations compete in global markets.

Impact of Tariffs in WTO:

- **Global Economic Integration**:
    o The reduction of tariffs under the WTO framework has been instrumental in the massive expansion of global trade, driving economic growth and increasing market access for developing nations.
    o Developing countries have benefited from preferential tariff reductions, giving them a

greater opportunity to export goods to wealthier nations.

- **Dispute Settlement Mechanism**:
    - The WTO has a robust dispute settlement system that allows countries to challenge unfair tariffs or trade practices. For instance, if one country imposes tariffs that violate WTO rules, another country can bring a case to the WTO, which can authorize sanctions if the rules are not followed.

Conclusion

Tariffs in international trade agreements, such as NAFTA/USMCA and the WTO, are used both as tools to promote trade liberalization and as instruments of protectionism for sensitive sectors. These agreements generally work toward reducing tariffs to encourage trade flows, while still allowing countries to protect specific industries from excessive foreign competition. The result is a balancing act that aims to foster global trade while managing national interests, economic priorities, and political pressures.

How Different Countries Respond to Tariffs

Countries around the world respond to tariffs in various ways, depending on their economic priorities, political interests, and strategic goals. The response to tariffs can be both direct and indirect, with governments and businesses adopting diverse approaches to mitigate the impact of tariffs or to use tariffs as a leverage point in negotiations. Below, we explore how different countries typically respond to tariffs, focusing on both retaliatory measures and proactive strategies.

1. Retaliation and Counter-Tariffs

Many countries respond to tariffs by imposing their own tariffs on goods from the country that initiated the trade barrier. This retaliatory approach often leads to trade wars, where multiple rounds of tariffs escalate the tension between nations.

Example - U.S.-China Trade War:

- **China's Response to U.S. Tariffs**:
  In the ongoing trade conflict between the U.S. and China, both countries have implemented tariffs on hundreds of billions of dollars' worth of goods. China responded to U.S. tariffs on Chinese imports by imposing its own tariffs on U.S. products, including agricultural commodities like soybeans, pork, and corn.
    o The goal of China's retaliation was to pressure U.S. farmers and industries that relied on exports to China, such as automotive and technology sectors. This retaliatory approach aimed to disrupt U.S. businesses and garner

domestic support by demonstrating strength in negotiations.
- **Consequences**:
Retaliatory tariffs often have adverse effects on both economies, leading to higher prices for consumers, disruption in supply chains, and slower economic growth.

Example - EU's Response to U.S. Steel Tariffs:

- When the U.S. imposed tariffs on steel and aluminum imports in 2018, the European Union retaliated by imposing tariffs on a wide range of U.S. goods, including motorcycles, whiskey, and orange juice. The EU sought to protect its industries while pressuring the U.S. to reconsider its tariff policies.
- The EU's strategic retaliation aimed to minimize the impact on European consumers while highlighting the negative consequences of unilateral trade policies.

---

2. Seeking Trade Negotiations and Resolving Disputes

Many countries use tariffs as bargaining chips in broader trade negotiations, attempting to leverage them to secure better terms in future trade agreements or resolve long-standing trade disputes.

Example - Canada and Mexico in NAFTA Negotiations:

- **NAFTA (North American Free Trade Agreement) Renegotiation**:
In the 2017-2018 renegotiations of NAFTA, Canada and Mexico were keen to protect their industries from U.S. tariffs, especially those targeting the automotive and dairy sectors. During negotiations, Canada and Mexico

used the threat of retaliatory tariffs as a tool to force the U.S. to make concessions in areas such as agricultural trade.
- **Compromise**:
The outcome was the USMCA (United States-Mexico-Canada Agreement), where both Canada and Mexico secured better market access for dairy products and gained favorable terms for the auto industry. By leveraging the threat of tariffs, these countries were able to extract key benefits in exchange for trade concessions.

---

3. Diversification of Trade Partners and Supply Chains

In response to tariffs, some countries attempt to reduce their dependence on any single market by diversifying their trade partnerships and seeking new sources of imports. This strategy reduces the vulnerability of their economies to the imposition of tariffs and ensures continued access to goods and markets.

Example - China's "Belt and Road Initiative":

- In response to U.S. tariffs, China has strengthened its economic ties with other countries through its Belt and Road Initiative (BRI), which promotes infrastructure development and trade links across Asia, Africa, and Europe.
- This strategic move allows China to reduce its reliance on U.S. markets while securing new trade routes and partnerships in emerging economies. By diversifying its trade relationships, China mitigates the impact of tariffs and opens alternative markets for its goods and services.

Example - European Union's Trade Deals with Asia:

- The European Union has increasingly focused on securing free trade agreements (FTAs) with countries in Asia, including Japan and South Korea, to ensure market access for European exporters. In response to rising protectionism globally, the EU has positioned itself as a champion of open trade, signing deals to reduce tariffs and facilitate cross-border investments in key sectors.

---

4. Domestic Support for Affected Industries

Countries often provide domestic support, such as subsidies, tax breaks, or government bailouts, to industries impacted by tariffs. This ensures that domestic producers can maintain competitiveness despite the rising costs imposed by foreign tariffs.

Example - U.S. Tariff Assistance to Farmers:

- When U.S. farmers were hit by tariffs on agricultural exports during the trade war with China, the U.S. government provided financial relief packages, including direct subsidies, to offset the losses. These support measures were intended to help farmers weather the storm, maintain their production levels, and stay afloat while the tariff dispute was ongoing.
- However, such support packages are often controversial, with critics arguing that they simply delay the inevitable adjustment and lead to inefficiencies in the economy.

---

5. Adjusting National Policies to Absorb Costs

Some countries respond to tariffs by adjusting their national economic policies to minimize the impact on both businesses and consumers. This includes reducing non-tariff barriers to trade, increasing domestic production efficiency, or lowering taxes to offset higher costs.

Example - India's Response to U.S. Tariffs on Steel:

- India has responded to tariffs on its steel exports by boosting domestic production capacity and increasing investment in local infrastructure. This allows Indian companies to reduce their dependence on exports and focus on domestic demand.
- The Indian government has also provided incentives to steel producers to modernize and enhance efficiency, helping them to remain competitive despite higher costs resulting from tariffs on exports to the U.S.

Conclusion

Countries' responses to tariffs depend on their specific economic needs, political goals, and strategic priorities. Whether through retaliation, negotiation, diversification, domestic support, or policy adjustments, nations have developed various tactics to minimize the impact of tariffs on their economies. The goal for most countries is to find a way to maintain or grow trade relationships while safeguarding their domestic industries and consumers. Understanding these responses helps businesses, governments, and consumers navigate the complexities of international trade in an increasingly tariff-impacted world.

The Ripple Effects of Major Tariff Disputes on Global Supply Chains

Tariff disputes, especially between major economic powers, can have far-reaching consequences on global supply chains. As countries impose tariffs on imports and exports, businesses and industries face higher costs, disrupted production schedules, and altered trade flows. The ripple effects of these disputes can stretch across borders, affecting everything from raw materials to finished goods, and even influencing the structure of global trade itself.

1. Disruption of Cross-Border Trade

One of the most immediate and visible effects of a major tariff dispute is the disruption of trade between countries. When tariffs are imposed, the cost of imported goods rises, making them less competitive in foreign markets. This leads to a reduction in trade volume and affects companies that rely on cross-border supply chains.

Example - U.S.-China Trade War:

- During the U.S.-China trade war, tariffs were placed on a wide range of goods, from electronics to agricultural products. As a result, U.S. businesses that relied on Chinese-made components faced increased costs. Chinese manufacturers, in turn, struggled to maintain exports to the U.S. market, leading to supply chain slowdowns and higher prices for end consumers.
- This disruption caused companies in both countries to seek alternative suppliers or adjust their sourcing strategies, further complicating global supply chains.

2. Rising Costs and Increased Prices

Tariffs increase the cost of importing goods, which often leads to higher production costs for manufacturers. These increased costs can then be passed down the supply chain to consumers, resulting in higher prices for finished products.

Impact on Consumer Goods:

- As an example, when the U.S. imposed tariffs on Chinese electronics, companies like Apple faced higher costs for components like chips and displays. Although Apple initially absorbed some of these costs, it eventually raised the prices of some products to offset the increased tariffs.
- Consumers in both the U.S. and other countries affected by the dispute faced higher prices on a wide range of goods, including household items, clothing, and electronics, thus reducing their purchasing power, and affecting overall demand.

---

3. Shifts in Global Sourcing and Production Locations

When faced with high tariffs, many companies adjust their sourcing strategies to minimize the impact of the trade dispute. This may involve relocating production to other countries with lower tariffs or seeking alternative suppliers that are not impacted by the dispute.

Example - China's Shift to Other Markets:

- In response to the U.S. tariffs, some Chinese manufacturers have begun moving parts of their production to Southeast Asian countries like Vietnam, Thailand, and Indonesia, where labor costs are lower and tariffs on goods going to the U.S. are less punitive.
- Similarly, U.S. companies have sought suppliers in countries outside of China to avoid tariffs, leading to shifts in supply chain dynamics. For instance, companies like Nike and Dell have diversified their manufacturing base by increasing production in countries like Mexico, India, and Vietnam.

---

4. Supply Chain Reshuffling and Delays

Tariff disputes often result in the need for businesses to reassess their entire supply chain structure. This can lead to delays as companies work to find new suppliers, adapt to new logistical routes, and reconfigure their operations.

Logistical Challenges:

- As supply chains are reshuffled, logistics networks must be reconfigured to account for the new production and distribution locations. Companies may need to find alternative shipping routes, warehousing facilities, and transportation options.
- The COVID-19 pandemic highlighted the fragility of global supply chains, and tariff disputes only exacerbated these weaknesses. A rise in tariffs between the U.S. and China, for instance, caused a backlog of shipments at U.S. ports, contributing to global shipping delays and an increase in container prices.

- The relocation of factories and the search for new suppliers also led to production delays, forcing businesses to adjust their delivery schedules and inventory management strategies.

---

5. Impact on Small and Medium-Sized Enterprises (SMEs)

Small and medium-sized enterprises are often more vulnerable to tariff disputes than larger corporations, as they lack the resources to quickly adapt or absorb additional costs. Many SMEs rely heavily on imported components and raw materials to produce finished goods, and higher tariffs can undermine their ability to compete in global markets.

Example - Tariffs on Steel and Aluminum:

- The U.S. tariffs on steel and aluminum imports placed a heavy burden on U.S. manufacturers in industries such as construction, automotive, and consumer goods. Smaller manufacturers, who were less able to negotiate favorable terms with suppliers, were hit particularly hard.
- Some SMEs were forced to raise prices, reduce workforce sizes, or even halt production entirely, resulting in job losses and economic hardship. For many small businesses, the additional cost from tariffs could be the difference between survival and bankruptcy.

---

6. Strain on Multinational Corporations (MNCs)

For multinational corporations that operate in multiple countries, tariff disputes create additional challenges. These companies are forced to navigate a maze of different tariffs in each market, which can undermine their economies of scale and increase their operational complexity.

Example - Automotive Industry Response:

- The automotive industry is particularly vulnerable to tariff disputes, as it relies on complex global supply chains for the sourcing of parts and assembly of vehicles.
- For example, during the U.S.-China trade war, U.S. automakers that sourced parts from China faced higher costs and potential disruptions. Meanwhile, companies like Tesla and BMW, which manufacture cars in China for export to the U.S., faced significant tariffs that made their products less competitive in the U.S. market.
- To counter these impacts, many MNCs began adjusting their supply chains, moving production facilities to countries with more favorable tariff conditions or increasing local sourcing of parts to avoid tariffs altogether.

---

7. Long-Term Changes in Global Trade Relationships

Prolonged tariff disputes can lead to lasting changes in global trade relationships, as countries seek new trading partners, and businesses adapt to the changing global landscape. This reshuffling of trade relationships can have long-term consequences for global supply chains and the broader economic environment.

Example - Trade Diversification:

- In the aftermath of major tariff disputes, countries and businesses often look to diversify their trading relationships. This can lead to new trade agreements, shifts in the global balance of power, and the development of alternative supply chains that are more resilient to tariff disruptions.
- For instance, following the U.S.-China trade war, China deepened its trade ties with countries in the Asia-Pacific region through the Regional Comprehensive Economic Partnership (RCEP), a major trade agreement that further integrated economies in the region and provided alternatives to U.S. markets.

Conclusion

The ripple effects of major tariff disputes are felt throughout global supply chains, affecting everything from production schedules and raw material costs to consumer prices and market access. Companies are forced to navigate these disruptions by adjusting their sourcing strategies, reconfiguring supply chains, and seeking alternative markets. The long-term consequences can reshape global trade relationships, making it essential for businesses to stay agile and adaptable in an increasingly tariff-impacted world. Understanding and anticipating these ripple effects is crucial for minimizing the impact of tariffs on supply chain operations and maintaining business continuity.

Chapter 4: Surviving Tariffs as a Business

Strategies for Minimizing Impact of Tariffs

Tariffs can disrupt businesses in various ways, but there are several strategies that companies can implement to minimize their impact. By diversifying supply chains, negotiating with suppliers, and investing in local production, businesses can better navigate the challenges posed by tariffs and protect their bottom line.

1. Diversifying Supply Chains

One of the most effective ways to mitigate the impact of tariffs is by diversifying supply chains. Relying on a single source or region for materials and components can make a business more vulnerable to disruptions caused by tariffs, trade restrictions, or geopolitical tensions. By sourcing from multiple regions and suppliers, companies can reduce their exposure to tariff-induced risks.

Key Tactics:

- **Global Sourcing**: Expand your supplier base to countries with favorable tariff agreements or low-cost production advantages. For example, if tariffs are imposed on Chinese goods, businesses can look to countries like Vietnam, India, or Mexico for similar products or components.
- **Regional Sourcing**: In some cases, sourcing from closer regions may help reduce transportation costs and tariff burdens. For example, U.S. businesses may shift their

sourcing from China to Canada or Mexico to take advantage of trade agreements like the USMCA (United States-Mexico-Canada Agreement).

By diversifying supply chains, businesses can avoid disruptions caused by tariffs affecting one specific country or region.

2. Negotiating with Suppliers

Establishing strong relationships with suppliers and negotiating favorable terms can help businesses manage the impact of tariffs. Suppliers may be willing to absorb part of the increased cost caused by tariffs, or they may offer alternative solutions to mitigate the impact.

Key Tactics:

- **Cost Sharing**: Negotiate with suppliers to share the burden of tariff-related costs. This may involve discussing price increases and determining how the costs will be distributed between the supplier and the buyer.
- **Alternative Materials**: Explore alternative raw materials or components that may not be subject to tariffs, thus reducing the overall cost impact.
- **Long-term Contracts**: Enter long-term contracts with suppliers to lock in prices before tariff increases take effect. This can help stabilize costs for an extended period, providing some financial predictability.

Effective negotiation ensures that businesses can maintain stable supply chains without absorbing the full brunt of tariff costs.

3. Investing in Local Production

Another strategy to minimize the impact of tariffs is to invest in local production. By manufacturing goods closer to the target market, companies can reduce their reliance on imports, avoid tariffs on foreign-produced goods, and potentially take advantage of local government incentives for domestic production.

Key Tactics:

- **Local Manufacturing Facilities**: Establishing manufacturing plants in key markets can help reduce the cost of imported goods and bypass tariffs on foreign-made products. For example, a U.S. company may consider opening a plant in Mexico to produce goods for both U.S. and Latin American markets.
- **Partnerships and Joint Ventures**: Partnering with local manufacturers or entering joint ventures can help businesses establish a presence in new markets while reducing tariff burdens.
- **Government Incentives**: Many countries offer tax breaks or other incentives to businesses that invest in local production. By taking advantage of these incentives, companies can offset the additional costs associated with manufacturing in a higher-cost country.

By investing in local production, businesses not only reduce their exposure to tariffs but also gain more control over their supply chain and production costs.

Conclusion

Minimizing the impact of tariffs requires proactive strategies and an adaptable business approach. Diversifying supply chains, negotiating with suppliers, and investing in local production are all effective tactics for managing tariff-related disruptions. By implementing these strategies, businesses can remain competitive in an increasingly complex global trade environment and protect their profitability against unforeseen tariff challenges.

Financial Planning:

Effective financial planning is essential for businesses to manage the costs and disruptions caused by tariffs. By budgeting for tariff-related expenses and exploring tax credits or government assistance programs, companies can safeguard their financial health and maintain operational stability in the face of increased costs.

1. Budgeting for Tariff-Related Costs

Tariffs can significantly affect a company's expenses, leading to increased costs for raw materials, finished goods, and logistics. Budgeting for these additional expenses is crucial to ensure that a business can maintain profitability without sacrificing quality or customer satisfaction.

Key Strategies:

- **Forecast Tariff Costs**: To prepare for tariff increases, businesses should calculate the potential financial impact based on the goods they import and export. Analyzing the tariff rates on key products and estimating how these will affect overall costs can help companies adjust their financial strategies accordingly.
- **Allocate Contingency Funds**: Setting aside contingency funds specifically for tariff-related costs is a prudent way to prepare for unforeseen expenses. This can be especially important if tariffs fluctuate unexpectedly or if new tariffs are imposed.
- **Adjust Product Pricing**: If tariffs significantly increase production costs, businesses may need to adjust their pricing strategy to reflect the higher cost of goods. Budgeting for this price adjustment should be part of

the financial planning process to avoid eroding profit margins.
- **Cost-Cutting Measures**: Businesses can offset tariff-related costs by identifying other areas where they can reduce expenses. This could include optimizing operational efficiency, reducing waste, renegotiating contracts with suppliers, or adopting lean manufacturing techniques.

By budgeting for tariff-related costs, businesses can better absorb the financial impact and continue operations without major disruptions.

2. Exploring Tax Credits or Government Assistance Programs

Many governments offer tax credits, incentives, or assistance programs to help businesses navigate the challenges posed by tariffs. These programs can reduce the overall financial burden on companies affected by tariff increases, allowing them to maintain profitability and competitiveness.

Key Strategies:

- **Tax Credits and Deductions**: Some governments offer tax credits or deductions for companies that face higher costs due to tariffs. For example, businesses may be able to claim tax relief for certain imports or receive credits for retooling manufacturing processes to comply with new trade regulations. Exploring these opportunities can significantly reduce a company's overall tax liability.

- **Government Subsidies and Grants**: In certain countries, businesses may qualify for government subsidies or grants aimed at mitigating the impact of tariffs. These programs can help businesses offset the additional costs of importing materials or transitioning to new suppliers.
- **Trade Adjustment Assistance (TAA)**: In some countries, businesses adversely impacted by tariffs may qualify for Trade Adjustment Assistance (TAA) programs. These programs provide financial assistance, training, and other resources to help businesses adjust to the changing economic landscape.
- **Export Credit Insurance**: Some governments offer export credit insurance to protect businesses from financial risks when exporting goods. This can be particularly beneficial when tariffs are imposed on exports, as it helps businesses secure payment and mitigate losses caused by trade restrictions.

By taking advantage of available tax credits and government assistance programs, businesses can ease the financial strain of tariff-related costs and stay competitive in a challenging global trade environment.

Conclusion

Effective financial planning is key to navigating the challenges posed by tariffs. By budgeting for tariff-related expenses and exploring tax credits or government assistance programs, businesses can better manage the financial impact of trade disruptions. These proactive strategies allow companies to remain resilient, maintain profitability, and continue to grow even in the face of tariff-induced challenges.

Tools and Technologies for Tracking and Managing Tariff Changes

As tariffs can fluctuate rapidly and impact a wide range of business operations, staying updated on tariff changes is crucial. Fortunately, various tools and technologies are available to help businesses track, manage, and adapt to evolving tariff regulations. These resources can help companies maintain compliance, avoid penalties, and make informed decisions that minimize financial disruption.

1. Customs and Trade Management Software

Customs and trade management software is a comprehensive tool for tracking tariffs, managing customs compliance, and ensuring that businesses adhere to all regulatory requirements. These platforms provide real-time data on tariff rates, customs duties, and trade restrictions across various countries, allowing companies to stay updated on changes that affect their operations.

Key Features:

- **Real-time Tariff Rate Tracking**: These systems update businesses on tariff rates as they change, ensuring that companies are always aware of the latest import and export duties.
- **Automated Customs Filings**: Some platforms allow businesses to automate the filing of customs documents, reducing the risk of delays or errors in tariff-related processes.
- **Global Compliance Tools**: With built-in compliance checks, businesses can ensure they meet the legal requirements of different countries when importing or exporting goods.

- **Tariff Impact Analysis**: These tools help businesses assess the impact of tariff changes on their supply chains and profitability, allowing for proactive adjustments.

Popular examples include **SAP Global Trade Services**, **Descartes Customs Info**, and **Integration Point**.

2. Trade Intelligence Platforms

Trade intelligence platforms provide insights into the global trade landscape, including detailed information on tariffs, trade policies, and market trends. These platforms aggregate data from multiple sources, including government agencies, international organizations, and trade associations, to deliver real-time information on tariff changes and trade barriers.

Key Features:

- **Comprehensive Trade Data**: These platforms collect and present tariff data from various countries, including import/export restrictions, tariffs on specific goods, and changes in trade agreements.
- **Custom Alerts**: Many trade intelligence platforms offer customizable alerts, notifying businesses when tariffs on specific goods change or when new trade policies are introduced.
- **Market Insights**: In addition to tariff data, these platforms often provide market analysis, offering insights into global supply chains and helping businesses identify new opportunities or risks.

Notable platforms include **IHS Markit Trade Data**, **Global Trade Tracker**, and **Import Genius**.

3. Automated Supply Chain Management Systems

Supply chain management (SCM) systems can be used to track and manage the impact of tariffs on global supply chains. Many modern SCM platforms integrate with customs and trade management tools, providing businesses with a holistic view of their supply chain, including tariff-related costs.

Key Features:

- **Real-time Inventory and Sourcing Data**: SCM platforms can track where goods are sourced from and their associated tariff costs, enabling businesses to quickly assess the impact of tariff changes on their supply chain.
- **Scenario Planning and Simulation**: Businesses can model different tariff scenarios within the SCM system to evaluate how tariff changes might affect inventory, sourcing, and production schedules.
- **Supply Chain Optimization**: SCM systems help businesses identify inefficiencies and gaps in their supply chain, enabling them to make adjustments in response to tariff increases or trade restrictions.

Popular SCM platforms include **Oracle SCM Cloud**, **Kinaxis Rapid Response**, and **SAP Integrated Business Planning**.

4. Global Trade Platforms and Databases

Several global trade platforms and databases offer businesses access to comprehensive tariff data, trade regulations, and compliance requirements. These databases allow companies to quickly search and access information on tariffs by product category, country, and region.

Key Features:

- **Searchable Tariff Databases**: Businesses can search tariff rates by Harmonized System (HS) code, enabling them to quickly identify tariffs on specific products.
- **Country-Specific Regulations**: These platforms provide detailed information on tariff policies, trade regulations, and customs procedures specific to different countries.
- **Trade Agreement Tracking**: Many platforms track international trade agreements and provide updates on tariff exemptions or reductions under specific agreements.

Popular platforms include **World Trade Organization (WTO) Tariff Database**, **U.S. International Trade Commission (USITC) Data Web**, and **Global Tariff Database by World Bank**.

5. Government Websites and Official Resources

For businesses operating in specific countries or regions, official government websites and resources often offer the most accurate and up-to-date information on tariffs and trade regulations. These websites typically provide information on current tariffs, updates to trade policies, and other regulatory changes that may affect businesses.

Key Features:

- **Direct Access to Policy Changes**: Government websites often publish official notices and announcements regarding tariff adjustments or new trade policies.
- **Regulatory Guidelines**: These resources provide businesses with clear guidelines on how to comply with tariff regulations and navigate customs procedures.
- **Public Access to Trade Data**: Many governments provide open access to trade data, including tariff schedules and trade statistics.

Examples include **U.S. Customs and Border Protection (CBP)**, **European Union's TARIC Database**, and **China's General Administration of Customs**.

Conclusion

Tracking and managing tariff changes is essential for businesses to stay competitive and compliant in the global market. Using the right tools and technologies—such as trade management software, trade intelligence platforms, and supply chain management systems—can help businesses monitor tariff rates, assess their impact, and make data-driven decisions. By integrating these technologies into their operations, businesses can respond more efficiently to changes in global trade policies and safeguard their profitability in an increasingly complex international trade environment.

Chapter 5: Navigating Tariffs as a Consumer

How to Identify Tariff-Inflated Prices

Identifying tariff-inflated prices is crucial for businesses and consumers alike, as tariffs can significantly impact the cost of goods and services. By understanding how tariffs affect pricing, businesses can make informed purchasing decisions, adjust their pricing strategies, and maintain profitability. Consumers, on the other hand, can make more conscious purchasing decisions to avoid overpaying for tariff-impacted goods.

One of the simplest ways to identify tariff-inflated prices is to track the historical prices of products before and after a tariff is imposed. If the price of a particular good rises suddenly and disproportionately to other economic factors, it's likely that tariffs are contributing to the price increase.

How to Track Price History:

- **Look for Sudden Price Spikes**: If a product's price jumps sharply within a short time frame, especially when no major supply or demand changes are taking place, this can be an indication of tariff inflation.
- **Compare Similar Products**: If similar products from different countries or manufacturers show a price differential after a tariff is imposed, the increase may be due to tariffs. Products from countries not subject to the tariff may remain priced lower.

The supply chain plays a pivotal role in determining the final price of a product. Tariffs typically raise the cost of raw materials, parts, or finished goods from specific countries, which in turn can increase the retail price. By examining the supply chain, businesses and consumers can better understand where tariffs are affecting costs.

Key Steps to Examine the Supply Chain:

- **Identify Import Sources**: Determine where the product is sourced from and check whether those countries are subject to newly imposed tariffs. Goods imported from countries that have recently faced tariff hikes are more likely to experience price increases.
- **Investigate Supplier Changes**: If a supplier has changed its prices or suppliers without any apparent changes in market demand, tariffs may be a contributing factor.
- **Review Shipping and Handling Costs**: Often, tariff-related price increases are passed along through higher shipping and handling fees. If there is a noticeable increase in shipping costs on imported goods, it could be due to tariffs.

If tariffs are being applied to imported goods, the prices of domestically produced alternatives may increase as well. This is often a result of businesses adjusting their pricing strategies in response to higher input costs caused by tariffs on imported materials.

Steps to Compare Domestic vs. Imported Goods:

- **Identify Similar Products**: Compare domestic products that don't face tariffs with imported counterparts that do. Look for price disparities and note whether they are consistent with the tariff increases.
- **Consider Domestic Manufacturing Costs**: If domestic manufacturers rely on imported materials subject to tariffs, their production costs could also rise. This may cause domestic products to rise in price even if they're not directly affected by the tariff on imports.

For businesses, analyzing the Cost of Goods Sold (COGS) can reveal the hidden impact of tariffs on product pricing. Tariff-inflated prices are often reflected in the COGS, which includes the cost of raw materials, labor, and manufacturing expenses.

How to Analyze COGS for Tariff Impact:

- **Review Cost Increase in Tariff-Affected Goods**: If the COGS of a product from a particular country has risen due to tariff increases, businesses may be forced to increase the retail price to maintain profit margins.
- **Check Product-Specific Costs**: Businesses can calculate how much of the price increase is directly attributable to tariffs by identifying cost changes in the raw materials or components that are imported from countries with tariffs.

Keeping track of trade policies, tariffs, and market trends through news reports, government announcements, and industry-specific publications can provide valuable insight into whether tariffs are inflating product prices. This information helps businesses and consumers stay ahead of price changes related to tariffs.

How to Assess Market Trends:

- **Follow Trade Policy Announcements**: Monitor government websites and international trade organizations for updates on tariff impositions and changes. These reports often provide details on the goods and industries most affected.
- **Review Industry-Specific Reports**: Many industries publish market reports that include tariff-related price impacts. These reports often contain analysis of how

tariffs affect both suppliers and consumers in various sectors.

Online price comparison tools allow consumers and businesses to track price fluctuations across different retailers and regions. By using these tools, individuals can spot when prices spike due to tariffs, especially if the price of a specific product is significantly higher in regions affected by tariffs.

Steps to Use Price Comparison Tools:

- **Track Multiple Retailers**: Use online platforms like **Google Shopping, PriceGrabber**, or to compare prices for the same product across different stores. Price discrepancies across regions can highlight where tariffs are impacting prices.
- **Set Price Alerts**: Some tools allow users to set price alerts for products, notifying them when the price exceeds a certain threshold, which can help identify when a tariff increase has caused a significant price hike.

Conclusion

Identifying tariff-inflated prices involves a combination of research, market observation, and analysis of the supply chain. By tracking product price history, examining supply chains, comparing domestic and imported goods, analyzing COGS, staying informed on market trends, and using price comparison tools, both businesses and consumers can gain insight into how tariffs are influencing prices. This understanding allows for more informed purchasing decisions, better budgeting, and more strategic business pricing to mitigate the effects of tariff-induced cost increases.

Strategies for Saving Money: Alternative Brands, Local Goods, and More

In an environment where tariffs are driving up the cost of goods, consumers and businesses alike need to adopt creative strategies to manage expenses. By exploring alternative brands, sourcing local products, and employing other cost-saving tactics, you can minimize the impact of inflated prices and protect your budget.

One of the simplest ways to save money when faced with rising prices due to tariffs is to switch to alternative or generic brands. Many generic or store-brand products offer the same quality as name-brand items but at a fraction of the cost.

How to Save:

- **Compare Ingredients and Specifications**: Before opting for a name brand, check the ingredients or product specifications. Generic or alternative brands may have similar quality or features, meaning you're not sacrificing much for the price difference.
- **Buy in Bulk**: Many generic brands offer larger package sizes at better value, especially if you're purchasing everyday items like food, cleaning supplies, or personal care products.
- **Look for Sales and Promotions**: Even alternative or generic brands often go on sale, allowing you to save even more. Take advantage of coupons, loyalty programs, and seasonal discounts.

Tariffs typically apply to imports, which makes domestically produced goods a cost-effective alternative.

By choosing locally sourced products, you can avoid additional costs related to import tariffs and support local businesses at the same time.

How to Save:

- **Support Local Farmers and Artisans**: Instead of purchasing imported goods, look for locally grown produce, locally manufactured goods, or handmade items. These products often cost less due to the absence of import duties and long-distance shipping costs.
- **Shop at Farmers' Markets or Local Retailers**: Farmers' markets and local stores may carry products that have avoided tariffs, offering more competitive prices for fresh produce, meats, dairy, and other goods.
- **Prioritize Domestic Products**: Many countries incentivize the purchase of domestic products through tax breaks or subsidies, which can lower the price of locally produced goods.

In some cases, opting for smaller quantities or less expensive versions of a product can reduce the impact of tariff-induced price hikes. This approach can be particularly effective with items where bulk sizes are subject to tariffs, but smaller sizes are not as heavily affected.

How to Save:

- **Buy Smaller Sizes**: For items like electronics, household goods, or cleaning supplies, purchasing a smaller size can help reduce costs. Often, larger packages or bulk items may carry a higher per-unit cost due to the added tariff burden.
- **Downsize Purchases**: If you don't need a large quantity of a product, downsizing to a more affordable version

can help minimize costs. This is especially true for seasonal or non-essential items.

Many goods that are subject to tariffs can be substituted with DIY alternatives. Whether it's making your own cleaning products, repairing items instead of buying new ones, or cooking from scratch, taking a hands-on approach can significantly reduce the need for imports.

How to Save:

- **Make Your Own Household Products**: Instead of buying cleaning supplies or beauty products, consider making them at home with simple ingredients like vinegar, baking soda, or essential oils.
- **Home Repairs and Maintenance**: Rather than paying for expensive repairs or buying new products, consider fixing items yourself. There are plenty of tutorials and resources online to help you with basic home repairs, upcycling, and reusing materials.
- **Cook From Scratch**: Buying pre-packaged meals and imported ingredients can be expensive. Instead, try preparing meals from locally sourced, seasonal ingredients, which are often cheaper and healthier.

The internet has made it easier than ever to find the best deals on products, even when tariffs are increasing prices. By leveraging online tools and platforms, you can identify opportunities to save on the goods you need.

How to Save:

- **Use Price Comparison Websites**: Tools like **Google Shopping, PriceGrabber**, or help compare prices across multiple retailers to ensure you're getting the best deal.

- **Shop During Sales Events**: Look for online sales events like Black Friday, Cyber Monday, or seasonal clearances to buy products at reduced prices.
- **Use Cash-Back and Reward Programs**: Take advantage of online retailers that offer loyalty programs, cash-back deals, or discounts for bulk purchases.

Many items, particularly electronics and furniture, are available second-hand or refurbished at significantly lower prices. These products may be subject to fewer or no tariffs, allowing you to save money while still getting high-quality items.

How to Save:

- **Shop at Thrift Stores or Online Marketplaces**: Websites like **eBay, Facebook Marketplace,** or **ThredUp** offer second-hand products, often at a fraction of the retail price.
- **Buy Refurbished Electronics**: Many tech companies, such as **Apple** or **Dell**, offer refurbished models at a reduced price. These products are tested and certified to work like new but can be significantly more affordable.
- **Check Local Resale Shops**: Many areas have local stores specializing in second-hand goods, offering everything from furniture to appliances at discounted prices.

If you are unsure whether a product's price is inflated due to tariffs, it may be wise to delay your purchase until the market stabilizes. Over time, businesses may adjust their pricing in response to tariff changes, allowing for lower prices later.

How to Save:

- **Monitor Price Trends**: Stay informed about tariff-related news and trends in pricing. If you see that prices are temporarily higher due to tariffs, consider waiting for the price to drop once the tariff impact subsides.
- **Avoid Impulse Purchases**: Delaying unnecessary purchases can help you avoid paying inflated prices due to short-term market fluctuations caused by tariffs.

Conclusion

When faced with rising prices due to tariffs, adopting strategic purchasing behaviors can help you navigate these cost increases while maintaining a healthy budget. By opting for alternative brands, supporting local goods, embracing smaller quantities, using DIY solutions, shopping online for deals, purchasing second-hand items, or delaying non-essential purchases, you can save money and avoid being overwhelmed by tariff-induced price hikes. With a little planning and flexibility, you can continue to access the products you need without sacrificing your financial well-being.

Advocating for Fair Trade Practices

As tariffs and trade barriers continue to shape global commerce, advocating for fair trade practices has become more important than ever. Fair trade aims to create a more equitable economic system by ensuring that producers, workers, and consumers alike are treated justly. Whether you're a business leader, consumer, or policymaker, understanding and supporting fair trade practices can contribute to reducing inequalities, fostering ethical business practices, and creating more sustainable economic relationships.

Fair trade is an approach to international trade that focuses on creating equal opportunities for marginalized producers in developing countries, ensuring they receive a fair wage and work under safe conditions. It involves setting minimum price standards, preventing exploitative labor practices, and promoting environmentally sustainable production methods.

Key Elements of Fair Trade:

- **Fair Wages and Labor Rights**: Ensuring workers are paid fairly for their labor and work in safe, healthy conditions.
- **Environmental Sustainability**: Encouraging environmentally conscious practices that promote sustainable agriculture and minimize damage to natural ecosystems.
- **Community Empowerment**: Supporting local communities by investing in social programs, education, and healthcare through the proceeds of fair-trade products.
- **Transparency and Accountability**: Ensuring that companies and consumers are aware of the practices

that go into the production of goods, creating a transparent and accountable trade system.

Advocating for fair trade practices brings a wide range of benefits, not just for the workers in developing countries but also for businesses and consumers who adopt fair trade products.

For Producers:

- Fair trade provides fair wages and access to better working conditions, reducing exploitation and poverty.
- It encourages community-based initiatives, enabling producers to reinvest profits into local development, such as infrastructure, education, and health programs.

For Consumers:

- Consumers who purchase fair trade products can feel confident knowing their money supports ethical practices and sustainable growth.
- It allows consumers to be part of a global movement that promotes fairness and equity, driving positive change in the global economy.

For Businesses:

- Fair trade can improve brand image and build customer loyalty, as consumers are increasingly looking to support ethical companies.
- It helps companies ensure a reliable supply chain by forging long-term relationships with producers and farmers, reducing volatility and uncertainties.
- Many companies report that fair trade practices lead to increased consumer demand, as shoppers are more inclined to buy products they know have a positive social impact.

Advocating for fair trade practices involves both individual actions and larger systemic changes that impact global trade policies. Below are some ways to get involved:

Educate Yourself and Others: Knowledge is power. Understanding the principles of fair trade, the challenges it seeks to address, and the benefits it offers can help you advocate more effectively. Share this knowledge with friends, family, and colleagues to build a broader awareness of fair-trade practices.

Support Fair Trade Certified Products: One of the most direct ways to advocate for fair trade is to purchase products from fair trade-certified organizations. Look for the fair-trade logo on goods like coffee, tea, chocolate, clothing, and handicrafts. These certifications ensure that the product was produced under fair conditions and that the workers involved are treated ethically.

Encourage Businesses to Adopt Fair Trade Practices: Businesses, from small retailers to multinational corporations, have significant power in shaping trade practices. Encourage the businesses you interact with to adopt fair trade principles, either by purchasing fair trade goods or by working with suppliers who adhere to fair labor and environmental standards.

Advocate for Fair Trade Policies: Advocate for stronger trade policies at the national and international levels that promote fair trade practices and reduce harmful tariffs that disproportionately impact developing countries. Participate in campaigns or petitions that aim to support fair trade regulations.

Join Fair Trade Organizations: Many organizations work to support fair trade on a global scale, including the Fair-

Trade Federation and World Fair Organization. Joining these organizations, participating in their events, and donating to their causes helps drive the global fair-trade movement.

As a consumer your purchasing decisions can make a significant impact on fair trade practices. By consciously choosing to buy from companies and producers who adhere to fair trade standards, you are helping to create a demand for ethically produced goods. Here's how you can further contribute:

Advocate for Transparency: Encourage the companies you buy from to disclose their supply chain practices. Ask questions about the sourcing of their materials, labor conditions, and environmental impact. Transparency leads to accountability.

Support Local and Ethical Alternatives: When possible, choose locally produced goods or items from companies committed to fair trade principles. Local alternatives often reduce transportation-related emissions, and ethical businesses support more sustainable economies.

Demand Change from Policy Makers: Contact your government representatives to advocate for fair trade laws that prioritize the welfare of producers, workers, and the environment. Be vocal in supporting policies that aim to reduce exploitation and environmental degradation.

The fair-trade movement continues to grow as consumers become more conscious of their purchasing decisions, and businesses increasingly recognize the importance of ethical sourcing. However, much work remains to be done. Increasing global trade imbalances, income inequality, and environmental degradation necessitate a broader, more systemic approach to fair trade practices. By standing behind fair trade principles, advocating for policy change, and supporting businesses that prioritize people over profits, we can contribute to a fairer, more sustainable global economy.

Conclusion

Advocating for fair trade practices is a powerful way to influence the global economy and create positive social, environmental, and economic change. By understanding what fair trade means, supporting fair trade products, and pushing for policy reforms, you are playing an essential role in creating a more equitable world. Whether you are a consumer, a business, or a policymaker, you have the power to drive change and ensure that trade practices are fair, sustainable, and beneficial for everyone involved.

Chapter 6: The Future of Tariffs

Merging Trends in Global Trade Policies

The landscape of global trade is evolving rapidly due to shifting economic, political, and technological factors. Over the past decade, certain trends have emerged and are now converging to reshape international trade. Understanding these merging trends is crucial for businesses, policymakers, and consumers as they navigate the complexities of a modern, interconnected world economy. Below are key trends in global trade policies that are converging and influencing the future of commerce:

In recent years, many nations have turned toward more protectionist trade policies as a response to growing economic uncertainties and national security concerns. This trend has been driven by factors such as increasing domestic unemployment, concerns over national sovereignty, and growing populism. Tariffs, trade quotas, and subsidies have become more common tools used to protect domestic industries from foreign competition.

Key Examples:

- **U.S.-China Trade War**: The ongoing trade tensions between the U.S. and China have led to significant tariff hikes, disrupting global supply chains, and raising costs for businesses and consumers worldwide.
- **Brexit**: The United Kingdom's exit from the European Union has prompted changes in trade agreements, tariffs, and border policies, shifting the dynamics of intra-European trade.

Despite these protective measures, globalization continues to influence global trade policies, and the balancing act between protectionism and free trade remains a central theme.

With the rise of e-commerce, digital trade has become an increasingly important aspect of global trade. The rapid growth of online shopping, cloud services, and digital platforms is creating new opportunities for businesses to expand across borders without physical presence. However, this has also led to challenges related to data privacy, cybersecurity, and digital taxation.

Key Examples:

- **Data Localization Policies**: Some countries, such as China and Russia, have implemented data localization laws requiring foreign companies to store user data within their borders, which can complicate international operations.
- **Global E-Commerce Regulations**: Countries are looking at how to regulate digital goods and services, create tax policies, and manage cross-border data flows, leading to a rise in digital trade agreements like the WTO's E-Commerce negotiations.

Governments are striving to keep up with the rapid pace of technological advancements, leading to the formulation of new policies to govern digital trade and e-commerce.

As the effects of climate change become more pronounced, environmental concerns have increasingly become a focal point in global trade policies. Countries are recognizing that trade should not come at the expense of the environment and are incorporating sustainability measures into trade agreements. This includes environmental standards, carbon pricing, and commitments to reduce carbon emissions as part of trade deals.

Key Examples:

- **EU Green Deal**: The European Union has been a leader in integrating environmental goals into trade policies, introducing carbon tariffs on imported goods that do not meet certain environmental standards.
- **Sustainable Supply Chains**: International companies are under increasing pressure to ensure their supply chains are sustainable. The growing demand for eco-friendly products has influenced trade policies that incentivize green technologies and low-carbon goods.

This trend is pushing businesses and governments to develop policies that encourage sustainable practices while maintaining the flow of global trade.

In response to the uncertainty created by multilateral trade systems, countries have increasingly turned to bilateral or regional free trade agreements (FTAs) to foster closer economic ties. These agreements offer flexibility and quicker negotiations compared to the often-slow-moving processes at the World Trade Organization (WTO). Regional trade agreements, such as the Comprehensive and Progressive Agreement for Trans-Pacific Partnership (CPTPP) and the Regional Comprehensive Economic Partnership (RCEP), have gained traction in recent years.

Key Examples:

- **USMCA**: The United States-Mexico-Canada Agreement, which replaced NAFTA, reflects a shift toward more regionally focused agreements that emphasize digital trade, intellectual property, and labor rights.

- **RCEP**: The RCEP agreement, which includes China, Japan, South Korea, and several other Southeast Asian countries, is the world's largest trade agreement and highlights a move toward regional economic integration.

These FTAs are increasingly seen to address trade challenges quickly and effectively, especially as global trade becomes more fragmented.

Geopolitical rivalries are influencing global trade dynamics, as countries assert more control over their trade relationships, often using tariffs, sanctions, or embargoes as strategic tools. Trade wars, such as the U.S.-China dispute, have sparked global economic slowdowns and led to significant policy shifts in various regions.

Key Examples:

- **U.S.-China Trade War**: The trade conflict between the two largest economies has resulted in tariffs on hundreds of billions of dollars in goods, affecting global markets and encouraging other countries to reconsider their own trade policies with China.
- **Sanctions**: Economic sanctions are increasingly being used as a foreign policy tool, impacting countries like Russia and Iran and affecting their ability to engage in global trade.

These geopolitical tensions often lead to significant shifts in trade alliances, as countries seek to protect their strategic interests and adjust their trade policies accordingly.

While globalization has traditionally been the driving force behind trade liberalization, the recent trend toward regionalization is altering the global trade landscape. Many nations are looking inward, focusing on regional partnerships, and reducing dependency on global supply chains. Regionalization also includes the formation of economic blocs, which promote intra-regional trade and reduce barriers for member countries.

Key Examples:

- **Belt and Road Initiative**: China's Belt and Road Initiative is an example of regionalization, focusing on infrastructure and economic connections between China and countries in Asia, Europe, and Africa.
- **Regional FTAs**: Agreements such as the EU's single market and the African Continental Free Trade Area (AFCFTA) exemplify regional efforts to foster trade within specific geographical areas.

As global trade continues to face challenges from geopolitical factors and protectionist policies, regional trade agreements are emerging as a potential solution for maintaining the flow of goods and services.

Increasingly, human rights and labor standards are becoming integral to global trade policies. With growing attention on fair wages, safe working conditions, and the prevention of forced labor, countries and international organizations are incorporating labor rights into trade agreements and regulatory frameworks.

Key Examples:

- **Social Clauses in Trade Agreements**: The inclusion of labor rights in trade agreements such as the USMCA, which includes provisions to protect workers' rights in

Mexico, has sparked broader discussions on how trade can help improve labor standards globally.
- **Sourcing of Ethical Goods**: There is a growing demand for goods produced ethically, with fair wages and safe working conditions. This trend is influencing trade policies and driving changes in consumer behavior.

This merging trend highlights the importance of aligning global trade policies with human rights, ensuring that economic growth benefits both workers and businesses.

Conclusion

The merging trends in global trade policies—protectionism, digital trade, sustainability, free trade agreements, geopolitical tensions, regionalization, and labor rights—are reshaping how nations interact with each other and how global commerce operates. As businesses, governments, and consumers navigate these evolving policies, staying informed about these shifts and adjusting strategies will be key to succeeding in an increasingly complex global marketplace.

The Potential for New Tariffs in Key Industries (e.g., Tech, Agriculture)

As global economic, political, and technological dynamics continue to evolve, new tariffs are emerging as a potential tool to address shifting trade relations and protect strategic industries. Several sectors, particularly technology and agriculture, are poised to experience increased scrutiny and the potential for new tariff implementations due to a variety of geopolitical, economic, and policy-related factors.

The technology sector has become a focal point in global trade disputes, as governments recognize its strategic importance for national security, economic growth, and innovation. With the increasing digitization of economies and growing reliance on technology infrastructure, new tariffs in this industry could have wide-reaching implications.

Key Drivers for Potential Tariffs:

- **National Security Concerns**: Governments are becoming more cautious about foreign influence in critical infrastructure, such as 5G networks, artificial intelligence, and semiconductors. Countries may impose tariffs or restrictions on technology imports from specific nations to protect sensitive sectors.

    Example: The U.S. has previously imposed tariffs on Chinese-made telecommunications equipment, citing national security risks with companies like Huawei and ZTE. These measures are being considered for broader tech industries as well.

- **Intellectual Property Protection**: Concerns over intellectual property (IP) theft and forced technology transfers could drive the implementation of new tariffs on high-tech products or components that are perceived to be involved in unfair trade practices.
- **Trade War Impacts**: The ongoing trade tensions between the U.S. and China have shown how tariffs can be weaponized in the tech sector, particularly in areas like electronics, computers, and mobile devices. There is potential for new tariffs to be imposed on these products as countries continue to assert control over their tech industries.

The agriculture industry is particularly sensitive to tariff policies, given the reliance on international trade for many agricultural products. Tariffs in the agricultural sector are often used as a tool in trade disputes, and their potential imposition can have significant consequences for both producers and consumers.

Key Drivers for Potential Tariffs:

- **Subsidies and Support for Domestic Agriculture**: Governments may impose tariffs on agricultural imports to protect local farmers from foreign competition and to support domestic agricultural industries, especially in times of economic uncertainty or overproduction.

    Example: The U.S. has historically used tariffs on agricultural imports like sugar, dairy, and livestock products to support domestic farmers. Similar measures could be expanded to address perceived unfair trading practices or domestic market imbalances.

- **Trade Disputes and Retaliation**: Agricultural goods are often a key focus of retaliatory tariffs in trade wars. As seen in the U.S.-China trade war, tariffs on agricultural products such as soybeans, pork, and wine were used by both countries to counterbalance other trade measures.
- **Climate Change and Sustainability**: With growing concerns over climate change, there is potential for new tariffs on agricultural imports from countries that do not meet environmental sustainability standards. These tariffs may focus on products that contribute to deforestation, excessive carbon emissions, or unsustainable farming practices.

The imposition of new tariffs on the tech and agriculture industries can have significant consequences for businesses and consumers alike.

- **For Businesses**:
    - **Increased Costs**: Companies that rely on imported tech components or agricultural products may face higher costs due to new tariffs, leading to higher production costs and reduced profitability.
    - **Supply Chain Disruptions**: For industries relying on global supply chains, new tariffs could create bottlenecks, delay product availability, and disrupt business operations, particularly for manufacturers that depend on foreign tech parts or raw agricultural materials.
    - **Market Shifts**: Companies may need to shift their sourcing and production strategies to mitigate the impact of tariffs, such as moving operations to countries with more favorable

trade agreements or investing in local production capabilities.
- **For Consumers**:
  - **Higher Prices**: Tariffs on tech products like smartphones, computers, and electronic devices could lead to higher prices for consumers, as businesses pass on the increased costs.
  - **Reduced Product Choices**: The imposition of tariffs on agricultural goods could limit product availability in some markets, leading to fewer choices for consumers and potentially reduced quality or variety in the marketplace.

The potential for new tariffs in key industries like technology and agriculture represents a critical shift in global trade dynamics. These tariffs could be imposed for a variety of reasons, including national security, intellectual property concerns, retaliation in trade wars, and sustainability objectives. For businesses, this could mean higher costs, supply chain disruptions, and shifts in market strategies. For consumers, the consequences could include rising prices and limited product choices. As these trends continue to unfold, stakeholders in these industries must be prepared to navigate the complexities of evolving tariff policies to stay competitive and adapt to changing global trade conditions.

How Businesses and Consumers Can Stay Informed and Adapt

Staying informed and being adaptable are essential strategies for both businesses and consumers when navigating the complexities of tariffs. With the ever-evolving landscape of global trade, knowing when and how tariffs are changing can mean the difference between success and struggle. Here are keyways businesses and consumers can stay informed and effectively adapt to tariff-related challenges:

For Businesses:

- **Subscribe to Trade News and Alerts**: Businesses should regularly follow trade publications, news outlets, and government websites that offer updates on tariff regulations and international trade agreements. Tools like the World Trade Organization (WTO) and regional trade bodies like the European Union's trade portal provide valuable resources.
- **Leverage Government Resources**: Many governments offer dedicated tariff databases, such as the U.S. Customs and Border Protection (CBP) or Canada Border Services Agency (CBSA), which businesses can consult for updates on tariff classifications, rates, and new regulations. Some agencies also provide alerts about tariff changes.
- **Consult Trade Experts and Legal Advisors**: It's beneficial for businesses to work with legal professionals or trade consultants who specialize in tariffs and international trade. These experts can offer advice on compliance, risk management, and effective adaptation strategies, ensuring businesses remain competitive.

For Consumers:

- **Follow Consumer Advocacy Groups**: Non-profit organizations focused on trade policies often provide useful insights into how tariffs may impact product prices and availability. These groups might also advocate for consumer-friendly policies and can be a source of information.
- **Track Price Trends**: Consumers can monitor the prices of commonly purchased goods over time through websites and apps that track price fluctuations. Sudden price increases may indicate tariff imposition on certain products, helping consumers make informed purchasing decisions.

For Businesses:

- **Adjust Pricing Models**: With new tariffs potentially increasing the cost of raw materials or goods, businesses may need to adjust their pricing models to reflect these changes. It's important to carefully evaluate whether to absorb increased costs or pass them on to consumers, weighing the impact on profit margins and customer loyalty.
- **Evaluate Supplier Relationships**: Businesses should regularly assess their suppliers to determine the impact of tariffs on the cost of imported goods. Exploring alternative suppliers from countries with favorable trade agreements or local options can help mitigate costs and reduce dependence on high-tariff regions.
- **Reevaluate Supply Chains**: Diversifying supply chains is one of the most effective ways to mitigate tariff risks. Businesses can consider reshoring or nearshoring manufacturing processes to reduce

reliance on international suppliers affected by tariffs, thus minimizing supply chain disruptions.

For Consumers:

- **Compare Prices Across Multiple Sources**: Consumers can stay ahead of tariff-related price hikes by shopping around and comparing prices from different sellers or retailers. Online platforms may also offer competitive pricing that mitigates the impact of tariffs in physical stores.
- **Consider Alternative Products**: If a product is subject to increased tariffs and price hikes, consumers can consider purchasing alternative brands or local goods that may be less affected by tariffs, potentially offering similar quality at a more affordable price.
- **Bulk Buying and Stockpiling**: When consumers anticipate significant price increases due to tariffs, they may choose to purchase in bulk or stockpile certain items in advance, especially for non-perishable goods, to avoid higher prices in the future.

For Businesses:

- **Lobby for Fair Trade Practices**: Businesses can engage with industry groups, trade associations, or government agencies to advocate for fair trade practices that protect their interests. By actively participating in trade policy discussions, businesses can help shape decisions about tariff implementation or reductions.
- **Collaborate with Other Businesses**: Forming alliances with other businesses in the same sector can amplify the voice for fair trade policies and

shared strategies for coping with tariffs. Collective advocacy can influence policymakers to reduce the impact of tariffs on critical industries.

For Consumers:

- **Support Consumer-Friendly Policies**: Consumers can advocate for transparent, fair-trade policies by engaging with organizations and policymakers that focus on consumer rights and trade. By participating in petitions or campaigns, they can raise awareness about the negative effects of tariffs on everyday goods.
- **Stay Engaged in Public Discussions**: Consumers can attend public forums, town halls, or webinars hosted by trade groups or government bodies to stay informed about policy changes and voice their concerns. This ensures their voices are heard in the decision-making processes.

For Businesses:

- **Utilize Tariff Management Software**: Businesses can invest in tools and software that help manage tariff rates, track import/export data, and automate compliance processes. These tools provide real-time updates on tariff changes, ensuring businesses stay compliant and avoid penalties.
- **Adopt E-commerce and Digital Tools**: E-commerce platforms and digital supply chain management tools allow businesses to quickly pivot and adjust to tariff changes by offering alternative sourcing options or accessing new markets that may be more tariff friendly.

For Consumers:

- **Use Price Comparison Tools**: There are various online price comparison websites and apps that track the best deals, including those impacted by tariffs. These platforms allow consumers to quickly assess where tariffs may have inflated prices and find alternatives that meet their needs.
- **Track Tariff Impacts Through Apps**: Some mobile apps are designed to help consumers monitor and compare the impacts of tariffs on products in specific industries, such as electronics, clothing, and food. Using these apps, consumers can stay informed and make purchasing decisions accordingly.

Staying informed and adaptable in the face of tariffs is essential for both businesses and consumers. Businesses can leverage trade news, government resources, and supplier relationships to minimize risks, while consumers can use price comparison tools, alternative product options, and advocacy to mitigate the effects of tariff-induced price increases. By taking a proactive approach to understanding tariff changes and adapting accordingly, both businesses and consumers can protect their interests and thrive in an evolving global trade environment.

Chapter 7: Real-World Survival Stories

Case Studies of Businesses That Thrived Despite Tariffs

While tariffs can present significant challenges, some businesses have successfully navigated these obstacles and even thrived. By adopting innovative strategies, diversifying supply chains, and leveraging local production, these companies have managed to turn tariff-related challenges into growth opportunities. Below are a few case studies of businesses that have flourished despite the imposition of tariffs.

Challenge:
Apple, one of the world's largest technology companies, faced substantial tariff challenges, particularly during the U.S.-China trade war. The U.S. imposed tariffs on Chinese-made electronics and components, including many of Apple's products, which significantly impacted the company's bottom line due to its reliance on Chinese manufacturing.

Response and Strategy:

- **Shifting Production**: Apple responded by diversifying its supply chain. The company began moving some of its production out of China to countries like India and Vietnam to reduce its exposure to tariffs. Apple also increased its investment in local production in the U.S., aligning with the Trump administration's push for American manufacturing.
- **Cost Absorption and Innovation**: Instead of passing the entire cost increase from tariffs onto consumers, Apple

absorbed some of the added costs and focused on introducing higher-margin products, such as premium models of the iPhone, to maintain profitability.

Outcome:
Despite the tariff impositions, Apple continued to report strong revenues, driven by its ability to innovate, diversify production, and retain a loyal customer base. Its proactive approach to mitigating tariff risks allowed the company to maintain its market dominance and keep its brand image intact.

Challenge:
In 2018, the European Union imposed tariffs on U.S.-made motorcycles as a response to U.S. steel and aluminum tariffs, which resulted in a 31% tax on American-made motorcycles exported to the EU. Harley-Davidson faced the risk of losing a significant portion of its European market due to the increased price of its motorcycles.

Response and Strategy:

- **Relocation of Manufacturing**: Harley-Davidson shifted part of its production overseas to mitigate the impact of tariffs on European sales. The company set up a manufacturing plant in Thailand to produce motorcycles for the European market, thus avoiding the hefty tariffs.
- **Focus on International Markets**: Recognizing the importance of global markets, Harley-Davidson increased its focus on international expansion, not only in Europe but also in other regions such as Asia, where tariffs were less of an obstacle. By strengthening its brand presence in new markets, the company balanced the impact of tariff-related price hikes.

Outcome:
While Harley-Davidson faced short-term challenges, the long-term strategy to shift production overseas and expand into international markets helped the company continue its global growth. The company's strategic moves allowed it to maintain profitability despite tariffs and strengthen its position in key markets.

Challenge:
Toyota, a global automotive manufacturer, faced the impact of tariffs imposed by the U.S. on imported vehicles from Japan and other countries. These tariffs increased the cost of importing vehicles and parts, affecting Toyota's profit margins, especially in its largest market—the United States.

Response and Strategy:

- **Localized Production**: To avoid the impact of tariffs on imports, Toyota expanded its manufacturing presence in the U.S. By increasing the number of cars and components produced locally, Toyota minimized its reliance on imports and reduced the tariffs it had to pay.
- **Investment in U.S. Plants**: The company invested heavily in U.S.-based manufacturing plants, building new production facilities in key states. This move not only allowed Toyota to sidestep tariffs but also helped the company create jobs and strengthen its relationships with American consumers.

Outcome:
Toyota's strategy of localizing production and expanding U.S.-based operations allowed it to maintain its competitive pricing in the U.S. market, despite the tariffs. As a result, Toyota continued to thrive in its key markets and even increased its market share in the U.S., with production costs lowered and tariffs minimized.

Challenge:
Tyson Foods, one of the largest U.S. meat producers, was caught in the middle of the U.S.-China trade war. China, one of the largest importers of U.S. pork, imposed tariffs on U.S. pork products, severely affecting Tyson's exports to the region.

Response and Strategy:

- **Diversifying Exports**: Tyson Foods quickly pivoted by finding new markets for its pork products, such as Southeast Asia, where demand for U.S. pork was on the rise. By focusing on regional diversification, Tyson was able to reduce its dependence on the Chinese market.
- **Leveraging Domestic Growth**: At the same time, Tyson focused on growing its domestic market presence. It increased its sales of processed meat products within the U.S., targeting both retail and foodservice sectors.

Outcome:
Tyson successfully mitigated the impact of Chinese tariffs through rapid diversification of export markets and a stronger focus on domestic growth. As a result, Tyson Foods not only weathered the trade war but also continued to grow its revenues and maintain a strong position in the global food market.

Challenge:
Lenovo, a Chinese multinational technology company, found itself affected by the U.S.-China trade war, with tariffs levied on computers and related electronics. This posed a serious risk to Lenovo's profitability in the U.S., its largest market outside of China.

Response and Strategy:

- **Manufacturing Shifts**: Lenovo made strategic shifts in its production facilities, moving a significant portion of its manufacturing outside of China. The company expanded its operations in countries such as Mexico and India, where labor costs were competitive, and tariffs were lower.
- **Cost Optimization**: Lenovo also focused on cost optimization within its existing U.S. operations, increasing efficiency in manufacturing and distribution processes to absorb some of the tariff costs without passing them onto consumers.

Outcome:
Lenovo's ability to adapt quickly by shifting production and optimizing costs helped the company remain competitive in the U.S. market, even with tariffs in place. Despite the challenges posed by the tariff environment, Lenovo maintained its market position as a leading global provider of laptops and computing solutions.

Conclusion

These case studies illustrate how businesses across different industries have successfully navigated the complexities of tariffs. Whether through diversifying supply chains, shifting production, expanding into new markets, or optimizing costs, these companies found innovative ways to thrive despite tariff challenges. For businesses facing similar obstacles, these examples provide valuable lessons in resilience, adaptability, and strategic decision-making in the face of global trade shifts.

Lessons Learned from Past Tariff Battles

Throughout history, tariff disputes have shaped the global economic landscape, offering valuable lessons on the consequences of trade barriers and the strategies used to mitigate their impact. By analyzing past tariff battles, businesses, governments, and consumers can gain insight into how tariffs can affect economic stability and trade relations. Here are some key lessons learned from past tariff battles:

One of the most prominent lessons from past tariff disputes, particularly the U.S.-China trade war, is the lasting economic impact that tariffs can have on both domestic and global economies. While tariffs may offer short-term protection to certain industries, the long-term consequences often include:

- **Supply chain disruptions**: Increased costs of imported goods can lead to inefficiencies, forcing companies to either absorb costs or pass them on to consumers.
- **Higher consumer prices**: Tariffs on goods like electronics, steel, and food can drive up prices for consumers, making everyday products more expensive.
- **Global uncertainty**: Trade wars can create market volatility and uncertainty, making it harder for businesses to plan long-term strategies.

The U.S.-China trade war, for instance, led to significant fluctuations in commodity prices and changes in trade flows, with countries like Vietnam and Mexico benefiting from new trade routes while others, like Brazil, suffered from disruptions in agricultural exports. This underscores how interconnected the world economy has become and the far-reaching consequences of tariff battles.

Tariff wars often trigger retaliatory measures, leading to a cycle of escalating trade barriers. This was evident during the U.S.-China trade dispute, where each side-imposed tariffs on billions of dollars worth of goods. The retaliation didn't just affect the countries involved—it also rippled across the global market. Some key takeaways include:

- **Increased operational costs**: As countries retaliate with tariffs on goods, industries that rely on global supply chains face higher costs and longer delays.
- **Economic isolation**: Prolonged tariff battles can isolate markets and limit access to international customers, reducing global trade flow.
- **Innovation stifling**: The uncertainty of retaliatory tariffs discourages innovation and long-term investments, as companies may hesitate to expand operations or enter new markets due to fears of future tariff hikes.

The trade war between the U.S. and the European Union over steel tariffs serves as an example where both sides imposed punitive tariffs on each other's goods. The cycle of retaliation led to negative impacts on industries such as automotive manufacturing and agriculture, highlighting the risks of escalating tariff battles.

While tariffs may provide short-term leverage, diplomacy and negotiation are crucial for long-term economic stability. Past tariff battles have demonstrated that the most successful resolutions often come through negotiation rather than prolonged conflict. The successful negotiation of the **North American Free Trade Agreement (NAFTA)**, for example, helped the U.S., Canada, and Mexico avoid tariff disputes and set the foundation for smoother trade relations.

Lessons learned:

- **Flexibility in negotiations**: Flexible trade policies that prioritize win-win outcomes for all parties can reduce the chances of trade wars and ensure a fairer global trade environment.
- **Collaborative problem-solving**: In many instances, tariffs were reduced or eliminated when countries worked together to find mutually beneficial solutions, as seen in the **World Trade Organization (WTO)** negotiations.
- **Escalation avoidance**: Diplomatic channels, such as the WTO's dispute resolution mechanisms, can help avoid escalation and encourage peaceful resolution.

The resolution of the **U.S.-Canada softwood lumber dispute** through negotiated settlements rather than a series of escalating tariffs is an example of how diplomacy can create more sustainable solutions.

One significant takeaway from past tariff battles is how businesses can leverage technology and innovation to adapt to changing trade policies. When tariffs disrupt traditional trade routes, companies that invest in technology can find new ways to manage supply chains, reduce costs, and minimize tariff exposure. Key lessons include:

- **Automation and digital transformation**: Businesses that embraced automation in production and digital solutions for inventory management and logistics were able to adapt more quickly to tariff-related disruptions.
- **Sourcing flexibility**: Technology-enabled platforms and real-time data analytics allowed businesses to identify alternative suppliers and adjust their sourcing strategies faster.
- **Improved forecasting**: By using predictive analytics, businesses could better forecast tariff impacts and

adjust pricing, production schedules, and supply chain routes in advance.

The rise of **blockchain technology** in supply chain management, for example, has helped businesses more transparently track the origin of goods, which can help avoid tariff disputes related to trade violations or misclassification.

Another important lesson from past tariff battles is the value of market diversification. Companies that relied heavily on a single market or supply chain partner often faced the most significant challenges when tariffs were imposed. By diversifying suppliers, markets, and production locations, businesses can reduce their vulnerability to tariffs. Key strategies include:

- **Geographic diversification**: Expanding into new international markets can help businesses reduce the impact of tariffs in a single region.
- **Product diversification**: Companies that produced a broad range of goods were better positioned to withstand tariff disruptions, as they were not overly reliant on one product or category.
- **Localizing production**: Some businesses responded by moving production closer to their customer bases to mitigate tariff impacts on cross-border goods.

For example, when the U.S. imposed tariffs on Chinese electronics, many companies in the tech industry sought to move production to countries like Vietnam, India, and Mexico to maintain access to tariff-free or lower-tariff markets.

Governments have a critical role to play in mitigating the negative effects of tariffs on domestic industries. During past tariff battles, governments offered subsidies, tax breaks, or assistance packages to affected sectors. Some key takeaways include:

- **Trade relief programs**: Programs like the **U.S. Trade Adjustment Assistance (TAA)** provided financial aid and retraining for workers in industries harmed by tariffs.
- **Policy advocacy**: Lobbying for fair trade policies that support key sectors can help reduce the economic damage caused by tariffs.
- **Support for small businesses**: Smaller businesses that lack the resources to absorb tariff costs benefit from government intervention, including financial support or tariff exemptions.

The **EU's response to U.S. steel tariffs** is an example of government efforts to offer support to affected industries, helping them transition to new export markets or subsidize losses from trade restrictions.

Conclusion

Tariff battles have taught us several key lessons about the complexities of global trade. The long-term economic consequences of tariffs, the risks of retaliation, the importance of diplomatic negotiation, and the role of technology and market diversification are all essential factors for businesses and governments to consider when navigating trade policies. By applying these lessons, companies and policymakers can better prepare for the challenges posed by tariffs and work toward more sustainable, fair-trade practices.

Chapter 8: A Practical Survival Toolkit

A Step-by-Step Guide for Businesses

Managing the impact of tariffs requires proactive planning and effective strategies. Below is a step-by-step guide for businesses to navigate tariff risks, build a comprehensive tariff management plan, and leverage government resources and trade organizations to minimize the impact of tariffs.

The first step in preparing for the impact of tariffs is to conduct a thorough tariff risk assessment. This involves analyzing how tariffs could affect your business operations, supply chain, and cost structures. Follow these steps to conduct an effective risk assessment:

Step 1: Identify Tariff Exposure

- **Review trade flows**: Identify which products are imported or exported, and check the tariffs imposed on those goods in both domestic and international markets.
- **Assess tariff rates**: Look up applicable tariffs for each country and product. Tariffs vary significantly across regions, so it's crucial to check the specific rates for the countries you are involved with.

Step 2: Evaluate Supply Chain Risks

- **Map out your supply chain**: Trace the entire supply chain, from raw materials to finished goods, and assess how tariffs might increase the cost of production, materials, or shipping.

- **Analyze supplier vulnerability**: Identify suppliers that may be directly impacted by tariffs and determine whether you can source goods from alternative suppliers or regions.

Step 3: Forecast Financial Impact

- **Cost calculations**: Estimate how tariffs could increase the cost of goods sold (COGS) and the potential impact on your profit margins.
- **Scenario planning**: Develop financial scenarios to predict the impact of tariff increases on your business, including worst-case scenarios, and analyze how you can adapt your pricing structure.

Step 4: Evaluate Legal and Compliance Risks

- **Check compliance requirements**: Review your company's compliance with customs and tariff regulations, especially if you import/export goods regularly.
- **Legal consultation**: Consider consulting with trade lawyers to ensure you are following all necessary legal procedures in tariff-related matters.

Once you have conducted a tariff risk assessment, the next step is to develop a tariff management plan. This plan will help you prepare your business for the financial and operational impacts of tariffs.

Step 1: Set Clear Objectives

- **Establish business goals**: Define clear goals for minimizing the impact of tariffs, such as reducing tariff exposure, optimizing sourcing strategies, or increasing profitability despite tariffs.

- **Establish key performance indicators (KPIs)**: Develop KPIs to measure the success of your tariff management strategies. These could include cost savings from sourcing adjustments, tariff reductions through negotiation, or improvements in supply chain efficiency.

Step 2: Diversify Supply Chains

- **Evaluate alternative suppliers**: Identify potential alternative suppliers from countries that have lower, or no tariffs imposed on certain products. This could help minimize the impact of rising tariffs on your supply chain.
- **Consider nearshoring or reshoring**: Evaluate the benefits of moving production closer to your primary markets to reduce exposure to international tariffs. For example, reshoring production to North America or Europe can decrease reliance on countries subject to heavy tariffs.
- **Build supplier relationships**: Strengthen relationships with your suppliers to ensure they are also prepared for tariff changes and are actively seeking out cost-saving alternatives.

Step 3: Leverage Technology

- **Utilize tariff management software**: Invest in technology tools and software that can track tariff changes in real-time and automate the calculation of tariff costs, helping you stay updated and adjust your pricing models accordingly.
- **Data analytics**: Use data analytics to monitor market trends and forecast the long-term effects of tariffs on your business. Predicting changes in tariffs can help you stay ahead and adapt faster.

Step 4: Adjust Pricing Strategies

- **Price optimization**: Review your pricing strategy to offset tariff-related cost increases. Depending on your industry, you may need to adjust your pricing model to remain competitive while covering the increased costs of production.
- **Transparency with customers**: If prices increase due to tariffs, consider informing customers transparently about the reasons behind the price hikes, building trust and maintaining customer loyalty.

Step 5: Contingency Planning

- **Create contingency plans**: Develop contingency strategies for situations where tariffs unexpectedly increase, or new tariffs are imposed. Have alternative supply chain routes, additional suppliers, or production flexibility available to minimize the disruption to your operations.

Governments and trade organizations offer valuable resources that can help businesses mitigate the impact of tariffs. Leveraging these resources can provide financial assistance, legal guidance, and up-to-date trade information.

Step 1: Utilize Government Assistance Programs

- **Explore tariff relief programs**: Many governments offer programs to support businesses facing the effects of tariffs, such as **tax credits, subsidies,** or **trade adjustment assistance**. For example, the U.S. offers the **Trade Adjustment Assistance (TAA)** program to help workers and businesses that are negatively affected by tariffs.

- **Inquire about exemptions**: Certain businesses may qualify for tariff exemptions on specific goods. Check with local customs authorities to see if your business can apply for tariff relief based on your industry or product categories.

Step 2: Join Trade Associations and Industry Groups

- **Find relevant industry groups**: Join trade associations that advocate on behalf of your industry and offer resources to help businesses deal with tariffs. Groups like the **U.S. Chamber of Commerce** or **the National Association of Manufacturers** often provide policy updates and insights on tariffs.
- **Collaborate with peers**: Trade organizations often provide opportunities to collaborate with other businesses in your industry to address common concerns about tariffs and advocate for fair trade practices. This collective power can help influence policy decisions and promote favorable trade conditions.

Step 3: Stay Updated on Trade Agreements

- **Monitor trade negotiations**: Stay informed on international trade negotiations and tariff agreements that may affect your business. Organizations like the **World Trade Organization (WTO)** and **regional trade groups (e.g., NAFTA or EU)** are key sources of information.
- **Leverage free trade agreements (FTAs)**: Take advantage of any free trade agreements your country has signed that may offer reduced tariffs or exemptions. FTAs often reduce tariff barriers and improve market access for businesses in certain sectors.

Step 4: Consult with Trade Experts

- **Work with trade consultants**: Trade consultants and customs brokers can provide expert advice on navigating tariff policies, avoiding compliance issues, and identifying tariff reduction opportunities. Their insights can help your business reduce its exposure to tariff-related risks.
- **Engage with legal experts**: Consult trade lawyers to ensure your business is following changing tariff rules, and to explore legal avenues for appealing tariff decisions or seeking tariff reductions.

Conclusion

By conducting a thorough tariff risk assessment, building a strategic tariff management plan, and leveraging government resources and trade organizations, businesses can minimize the negative impact of tariffs and ensure they remain competitive in the global market. Proactive preparation, diversification, and informed decision-making are key to surviving—and thriving—despite tariff fluctuations.

A Step-by-Step Guide for Consumers

Navigating the impact of tariffs as a consumer requires thoughtful budgeting and a commitment to supporting sustainable products. Below is a step-by-step guide for consumers to manage the financial effects of tariffs and make informed purchasing decisions.

As tariffs increase the prices of imported goods, consumers must be prepared to adjust their budgets to accommodate these changes. The following steps can help you manage the financial impact:

Step 1: Track Your Spending

- **Review your current expenses**: Start by understanding where your money is going each month. Categorize your spending to see which areas might be most affected by tariff increases (e.g., imported goods like electronics, clothing, or food).
- **Identify tariff-sensitive items**: Look for products that are most likely to be impacted by tariffs, such as electronics, vehicles, or goods from specific countries. These items may see a price increase as tariffs rise.

Step 2: Adjust Your Budget

- **Set aside additional funds**: Increase your budget for goods that are directly affected by tariffs. For example, if the price of imported goods is rising, ensure you allocate more money for these expenses in your monthly budget.
- **Prioritize essential goods**: Focus on buying necessities first and avoid purchasing non-essential items that might experience price hikes. This will help ensure your

budget remains balanced while coping with price increases.
- **Consider long-term expenses**: While it's important to adjust in the short term, think about the long-term implications of tariff hikes. If tariffs on goods like cars, appliances, or electronics are expected to rise, it might be worthwhile to make purchases sooner rather than later to avoid higher costs in the future.

Step 3: Explore Cost-Cutting Strategies

- **Look for discounts or sales**: Keep an eye out for sales, promotions, and discount opportunities that can help offset the higher prices of tariff-affected products. Some retailers may offer deals to remain competitive despite rising costs.
- **Use price comparison tools**: Take advantage of online tools and apps that allow you to compare prices across multiple retailers. This can help you find the best deals on goods and make informed purchasing decisions.

While tariffs may drive up prices on certain goods, you can counteract this by prioritizing local and sustainably produced products. Supporting these products not only helps your budget but also contributes to a more resilient and environmentally conscious economy.

Step 1: Identify Local Alternatives

- **Seek out locally produced goods**: Look for items that are made domestically or within your region. These goods are less likely to be impacted by international tariffs, as they don't rely on overseas production or imports. By purchasing local, you support domestic businesses and help reduce the strain tariffs put on imports.

- **Visit local farmers' markets and artisans**: Farmers' markets and local artisans often offer goods at competitive prices without the added burden of import tariffs. You may find unique, high-quality products while supporting local economies.

Step 2: Focus on Sustainable and Ethical Products

- **Prioritize sustainable products**: opt for products made from environmentally friendly materials or through sustainable production methods. These items may have a slightly higher upfront cost but can help reduce long-term environmental impacts and support businesses with ethical practices.
- **Support Fair Trade certified goods**: Many products, especially food and clothing, are available through Fair Trade certification programs. These products ensure that workers receive fair wages and work under humane conditions, and they often come from regions where tariffs are less likely to affect prices.

Step 3: Consider the Total Cost of Ownership

- **Look beyond the initial price**: While some local and sustainable products may have a higher initial cost, they often provide long-term savings. Consider the total cost of ownership when making a purchase—items that last longer or are more energy-efficient can save you money over time.
- **Support products with warranties and guarantees**: Many locally produced items or sustainable brands offer warranties and guarantees, which can save you money on repairs and replacements in the future. Factor this into your purchasing decisions to maximize value.

Step 4: Advocate for Local and Sustainable Industries

- **Engage with local businesses**: Support businesses that prioritize ethical production practices and are transparent about their supply chain. Show your support by leaving reviews, sharing your experience on social media, and encouraging others to make similar choices.
- **Participate in sustainability efforts**: Get involved in local initiatives or sustainability movements that focus on reducing dependency on global supply chains. This can help reduce reliance on imported goods and minimize the effects of tariffs in your community.

By budgeting for increased costs and supporting local and sustainable products, consumers can reduce their exposure to the financial effects of tariffs while contributing to more resilient and ethical economies. Prioritizing thoughtful purchasing decisions and investing in sustainable goods not only helps manage the challenges posed by tariffs but also encourages long-term financial savings and positive environmental impact.

Conclusion

As tariffs continue to shape the global trade landscape, understanding their effects and implementing strategies to navigate them is crucial for both businesses and consumers. Throughout this guide, we have explored the fundamentals of tariffs, their far-reaching consequences, and practical approaches to minimize their impact.

- **Tariffs are complex tools**: They come in various forms, each serving specific political, economic, or social purposes. Understanding these nuances can help businesses and consumers make informed decisions.
- **Tariffs affect prices and availability**: Both businesses and consumers face increased costs due to tariffs, which can disrupt supply chains and raise prices on everyday goods.
- **Adaptation is key**: Whether you are a business owner diversifying supply chains or a consumer supporting local goods, being proactive in adapting to tariff changes is vital for mitigating their financial impact.
- **Global trade dynamics are fluid**: With international trade policies constantly evolving, staying informed is essential for anticipating new tariffs and adjusting strategies accordingly.

The world of global trade is in constant flux, and tariffs reflect broader economic, political, and social trends. By staying proactive—whether through regularly reviewing trade agreements, diversifying supply chains, or adjusting personal purchasing habits—businesses and consumers can better withstand the volatility of tariff fluctuations.

Adaptability is also crucial. As global trade patterns shift, those who can quickly pivot in response to changes in tariff structures will be better positioned to thrive. Whether it's investing in local production, shifting sourcing strategies, or planning for potential price increases, being flexible ensures that you can weather whatever challenges come your way.

Preparation is the key to thriving in an environment where tariffs are an ongoing reality. Here's how you can get ready for the next wave of tariff changes:

- **Stay informed**: Regularly monitor international trade news, government updates, and industry reports to stay ahead of any potential tariff changes that could affect you.
- **Assess your exposure**: If you're a business, conduct a thorough tariff risk assessment. If you're a consumer, consider which products or services in your budget are most likely to be impacted by tariff hikes.
- **Diversify your options**: For businesses, diversify your suppliers and production locations to reduce reliance on a single region. As a consumer, explore alternatives to imported goods, like local or sustainable products, to minimize cost increases.
- **Advocate for fair trade**: Engage with policymakers or trade organizations to promote fair and transparent trade practices that benefit both consumers and businesses.

By applying the strategies and lessons from this guide, you'll be better prepared to navigate the complexities of tariffs and position yourself for long-term success in an unpredictable global economy.

Appendices

1. **Tariff**: A tax or duty imposed by a government on imported or exported goods to regulate trade and protect domestic industries.
2. **Import Tariff**: A tax placed on goods brought into a country to make foreign products more expensive and encourage consumers to buy domestic goods.
3. **Export Tariff**: A tax on goods leaving a country, usually to limit the amount of exports and retain resources for domestic use.
4. **Protective Tariff**: A tariff intended to shield domestic industries from foreign competition by raising the cost of imported goods.
5. **Revenue-Generating Tariff**: A tariff designed to generate government revenue by taxing imported or exported goods.
6. **Quota**: A limit on the amount of a specific product that can be imported or exported during a set period, often used in conjunction with tariffs.
7. **Trade Deficit**: A situation where a country imports more goods than it exports, resulting in a negative balance of trade.
8. **Free Trade Agreement (FTA)**: A pact between two or more countries to reduce tariffs and other trade barriers to encourage international commerce.
9. **World Trade Organization (WTO)**: An international organization that regulates trade between nations, working to ensure that trade flows smoothly and predictably.
10. **Most-Favored-Nation (MFN) Status**: A trade status granted by one country to another, ensuring the latter gets the best possible tariff rates available.
11. **Anti-Dumping Duty**: A tariff imposed on foreign goods believed to be priced below market value,

often to protect local businesses from unfair competition.

1. **The World Trade Organization (WTO) Website**
   www.wto.org
   The WTO provides in-depth resources and research on global trade agreements, tariff policies, and the impact of tariffs on international trade.
2. **The U.S. International Trade Commission (USITC)**
   www.usitc.gov
   A resource for U.S. tariff rates, trade policies, and research reports on trade impact.
3. **World Bank – Trade & Competitiveness**
   www.worldbank.org
   The World Bank offers extensive research, reports, and data on global trade and tariffs, along with insights into their effects on development and competitiveness.
4. **National Tariff Database (U.S.)**
   www.tariffdata.com
   A comprehensive database for U.S. tariffs and import/export data, helpful for businesses managing international trade.
5. **International Chamber of Commerce (ICC)**
   www.iccwbo.org
   Provides resources for businesses looking to navigate international trade, including trade policy guidance and trade-related dispute resolution.
6. **Global Tariff Finder (World Bank)**
   www.wto.org/english/res_e/res_e.htm
   This tool allows businesses and governments to track tariffs on products around the world.
7. **"The WTO and the Doha Round"**
   (Available in major bookstores and online platforms)

This book provides detailed analysis of the WTO and its impact on global trade policies.

1. Tariff Risk Assessment Template

Risk Factor	Impact on Business	Mitigation Strategy
Imported raw materials	Increased cost of production	Source locally, negotiate with suppliers
Finished goods from overseas	Higher retail prices	Identify alternative suppliers, explore local production
Foreign market access	Tariffs on exports, reduced demand	Diversify market channels, negotiate trade agreements
Global supply chain disruption	Delays, stock shortages	Establish alternative suppliers, increase inventory levels
Increased regulatory compliance	More time and resources needed	Stay updated on trade policies, invest in compliance tools

2. Tariff Management Plan Template

Company Name: [Insert Company Name]
Date: [Insert Date]

1. Overview
Outline of the company's current tariff-related risks and goals for tariff management.

2. Tariff Assessment
Identify the main products and raw materials affected by tariffs. This section should include details of affected imports, export destinations, and trade agreements in place.

3. Supply Chain Strategy
Define plans for diversifying suppliers and production locations. Consider shifting sourcing to countries with lower or no tariffs.

4. Financial Planning
Estimate the increased costs due to tariffs, and outline strategies for absorbing or passing on those costs to consumers.

5. Stakeholder Engagement
Communicate with suppliers, customers, and internal stakeholders about changes in tariffs and the company's strategy for handling these changes.

6. Government Resources
List any government programs, grants, or assistance available to businesses dealing with tariffs.

7. Review and Monitoring
Set up a schedule for regularly reviewing and adjusting the

tariff management plan based on changing global trade policies.

8. Key Performance Indicators (KPIs)
Define KPIs for monitoring the success of the tariff management plan, such as cost savings, on-time deliveries, and customer satisfaction.

By utilizing these resources and templates, businesses and consumers can stay informed and equipped to navigate the complexities of tariffs, ensuring that they are prepared for both the challenges and opportunities presented by an ever-evolving global trade environment.

Printed in Dunstable, United Kingdom

74468695R00067